STATE OF MISSOURI.

HOUSE OF REPRESENTATIVES.

City of Jefferson, March 18th 1872.

The University of Michigan presented with compliments of Henry Smith, M.A. of the class of '66 a Representative of the County of —— in the Missouri Legislature.

R. P. C. WILSON.

SPEAKER.

PEN-PICTURES

OF THE

OFFICERS AND MEMBERS

OF THE

HOUSE OF REPRESENTATIVES

OF THE

TWENTY-SIXTH GENERAL ASSEMBLY OF MISSOURI.

BY J. T. PRATT.

"Forsan et haec olim meminisse juvabit."—*Virgil.*

PRINTED FOR THE AUTHOR.

1872.

TO MY FRIEND

W. R. HARDIN, Esq.,

OF

PIKE COUNTY,

This unpretentious volume is respectfully dedicated.

PREFATORY.

The series of personal sketches contributed at random to the columns of one of the city dailies, during the regular session, will be recognized as constituting the nucleus of the present volume. To collate these and add others thereto has afforded the writer pleasant employment for the leisure hours of the adjourned session, and in returning them to the public in a more permanent form, he begs leave to say that he does so to gratify the wishes of a few personal friends, rather than any vanity of his own. He may also be permitted in this connection to return his thanks to Maj. T. O. Towles, of LaGrange, for the valued assistance on various occasions rendered him by that gentleman.

OFFICERS.

ROBERT P. C. WILSON,
(Speaker.)

Few possess in a more eminent degree the qualities that combine to make a good Speaker than the gentleman upon whom it has devolved to preside over the deliberations of the popular branch of the present Assembly. An accomplished parliamentarian, correct and always impartial in his rulings, an excellent judge of human nature, of suave and pleasant manners and at the same time of unmistakable firmness and decision of character, indispensable to the enforcement of order and discipline, it can be said without disparagement to any of his illustrious predecessors, that a better presiding officer has never been placed in the chair he occupies. The unanimity with which he was selected by his party associates upon the organization of the House was a compliment and mark of confidence in his abilities and fitness for the place, which his course since has shown to have been deservedly bestowed. As the first Democratic Speaker of the House since the war he has reflected scarcely more credit upon himself than upon the party to which he has been a lifelong adherent, and from which an acknowledgment of his faithful services was justly due. While a Democrat of the strictest school, however, I believe those who differ most widely with him politically, will agree with me in the assertion that so far as his course as an officer is concerned, he has in every instance ignored party and partisanship, and invariably shown that deference and indulgence due the minority of the body. Mr. Wilson is a native Missourian, and at present a resident of the populous county of Platte, which, with his worthy colleague, Mr. Ballard, he represents in the present House. After a thorough preparatory education he entered college at Danville, Kentucky, from which institution he graduated with credit at the early age of eighteen years. Upon completing his collegiate course he applied himself to the study of the law, which he soon mastered sufficiently to be admitted to practice. Immediately on receiving his law license he joined a party of his neighbors who were on their way to Texas for health and pleasure, and on reaching that State became infatuated with the free, wild life of the Southwest Texan border, and remained there until 1858, in the active and successful practice of his profession. Returning to

Missouri during that year on a visit, his friends induced him to remain. He then removed to the neighboring State of Kansas, locating at Leavenworth. Here he first entered the political arena, and in 1860 was elected to represent his county in the Kansas Legislature, being the Democratic nominee for Speaker of the House. Remaining in Leavenworth up to the close of the war, he returned to his native State and his old home in Platte county, where he has since resided. In January, 1863, Mr. Wilson was united in marriage with Miss Murray, of Platte county; a lady, distinguished not alone for her great personal beauty, but also for high intellectual endowments, and all those domestic virtues that go to make up the true woman. In 1866 he was solicited to become a candidate for the nomination for Congress from his district, and with this view canvassed a portion of it with the venerable Judge Birch, Geo. C. Bingham and Col. John Doniphan as competitors. It was during this canvass he established the high reputation he enjoys in the Northwest as being one of its most effective and brilliant orators on the hustings, having already taken the front rank as an advocate at the bar. He was taken sick however after having canvassed about half the district, and his illness being protracted, declined the canvass. From that time until the general election last fall he abstained from any participation in politics. He was then urged to become a candidate for the lower House of the present Assembly, which resulted in his election by perhaps the largest majority given to any member of the body. His course since his arrival at the Capital is well known. Chosen by the unanimous voice of his Democratic associates in the House to preside over their deliberations, he has applied himself to the discharge of the task imposed upon him with fidelity and that energy for which he is characterized. Mr. Wilson is peculiarly Western in manner and address, as he is in all his instincts. Tasteful, but plain in dress, with a countenance expressive of all the more prominent traits of his character—keen perception, indomitable will and determination strangely combined with a good nature and a pleasant expression—there are very few who have ever filled the chair with greater grace or efficiency, or who give higher promise of future usefulness to the State and nation.

CYRUS H. FROST,

(Speaker pro tem.)

Mr. Frost, Speaker *pro tem* of the House, is the Representative from Phelps county and chairman of the Committee on Mines and Mining. He has proven himself a valuable aid to Speaker Wilson in adjusting and keeping in running order the parliamentary machinery of the House. His rulings, like those of the latter gentleman, are invaribly governed by liberality of political sentiment, good judgment and a desire to conform strictly to the rules. The important measures that have been intrusted to his committee, namely: the establishing of a mining bureau and the measure to authorize the leasing of the agricultural lands donated by Congress, so as to render them available for the education of the youth of the State—have been promptly reported and passed, and the Representative from Phelps has thus fulfilled the special obligations which have attached to him growing out of measures affecting so directly the school of mines located at Rolla. But in the passage of all laws of a general character he has taken an active and prominent part, and his opinions always carry with them weight and influence. Mr. Frost was born in Jessamine county, Kentucky, in February, 1816, and is consequently 55 years of age. His father emigrated to Missouri in 1821. He has been almost constantly in public life since 1837, commencing with the offices of county assessor and sheriff in Crawford county. In 1844 he removed to Texas county, where he again filled the office of sheriff for four years, and was elected a Representative to the Legislature, a trust he filled with marked ability for four successive terms. Becoming wearied of the onerous duties imposed upon him at the State capital, he refused further nomination and was elected county court clerk, which office he held until 1862. At the outbreak of the war he removed to Rolla, Phelps county, and in November of that year was chosen State Senator from the Twenty-second district, filling that position with credit for four years. During the interim between that date and the last general election, he has been engaged in private business at Rolla, emerging from his retirement to accept the Liberal nomination for Representative. Mr. Frost commenced life without money or education, and his experience present a notable example of what energy and application will do in gaining a competence and securing the honors of public office. The affability of manner and uniform kindness which mark his intercourse with his fellow members have made him one of the most popular Representatives upon the floor.

D. A. SUTTON,

(CHIEF CLERK.)

Mr. Sutton, the efficient Chief Clerk of the House, is a New Yorker, having been born in Westchester county, in that State, March 17th, 1838. After completing his education at the Wesleyan University, of Connecticut, in 1858 he became connected with the newspaper press in New York city where he remained up to 1865, when he removed to Missouri to accept a position on the St. Louis *Times*, when that now flourishing Democratic journal was in its infancy. The services rendered the party in this connection, and especially his active participation in the canvass of 1870, secured for him, on the organization of the present House, the high compliment of the Chief Clerkship of that body, a position which he has proven himself peculiarly qualified to fill. Possessing a voice of great natural strength and clearness, which, by cultivation, has been rendered thoroughly under control, he has especially distinguished himself for his excellent reading at the desk, and thereby facilitated in no small degree the business of the session. With his fine elocutionary powers he also combines all the other qualities which go to render him "the right man in the right place."

W. C. B. GILLESPIE,

(ENROLLING CLERK.)

Maj. Gillespie was born in Cumberland county, Pennsylvania, in December, 1830, and during his boyhood removed with his parents to Muskingum county, Ohio, where he was raised and educated, and where he continued to reside until 1854, when he removed to Illinois and commenced teaching a public school. In 1857 he was elected Assistant Chief Clerk of the Illinois House of Representatives. In July, 1861, he enlisted as a private in the 41st Regiment of Illinois Infantry, was promoted to the Adjutancy in March, 1862, and was assigned to duty as Brigade Quartermaster in the same year, in which capacity he continued to serve until July, 1864, when he was mustered out of service. Within thirty days, however, he received a commission as Commissary with the rank of Captain, and was assigned to duty in Gen. Custar's Cavalry Division, where he served to the close of the war, being promoted to the rank of Major by Brevet for meritorious and efficient service. In 1865 Maj. Gillespie settled in Macon City, Missouri, where he has since resided. Under President Johnson's administration he was Assistant Assessor of Internal Revenue for that district. He has always been an unwavering, consistent and energetic Democrat, and has been a constant contributor to the political press of the country since he was eighteen years old, and is now the editor of both the Macon *Times* and the Kirksville *Register*, two of the most influential papers in North Missouri. He was elected to his present position upon the organization of the House in January, 1871, a position to which he is not only justly entitled on account of his valuable party services, but more especially by reason of his personal qualifications and fitness for the office.

J. L. DETCHEMENDY,
(Engrossing Clerk.)

Mr. Detchemendy, elected at the inception of the present session to fill the vacancy in the Engrossing Clerkship of the House occasioned by the death of Mr. Matthews, is a native Missourian, having been born in Ste. Genevieve county, April 13th, 1823, of French parents. After receiving only five months of English schooling he was placed when a boy an apprentice to the saddler's trade, at which he continued until he had reached the age of seventeen. After following this calling for some four years he commenced the study of the law, and in 1849 was admitted to the bar. On the organization of the Twentieth General Assembly he was elected Enrolling Clerk of the House, a position to which he was unanimously re-elected at the extra session of the same body in February, 1861. He subsequently served also as Journal Clerk in the Twenty-first Assembly. No member of the clerical department of the present body more fully comprehends the duties devolving upon him, or has applied himself more assiduously to their faithful performance.

J. D. CRAFTON,
(Sergeant-at-Arms.)

Col. Crafton, on whom it has especially devolved to preserve order in the hall, and who has proven a most valuable aid to Speaker Wilson in enforcing the mandates of the House, is a native of the Old Dominion, in which glorious commonwealth he was born in 1824. Leaving his native State in 1837 he immigrated to Mississippi, where he remained up to 1840, when he removed to Kentucky. From the latter State he entered the service at the outbreak of the Mexican war, throughout which he served as a Kentucky volunteer. In 1856 he removed to Missouri, but after a brief sojourn here made his way to Kansas, where he served as a member of the Territorial and subsequently of the first State Legislature of that State. Shortly after this he removed to Colorado, of which territory he was one of the original settlers. Here he also served one term in the Territorial Legislature. Returning to Missouri in 1866 he settled in Kansas City, where he has since continued to reside. Politically a zealous and uncompromising Democrat, he is nevertheless equally popular on both sides of the chamber, his course since at the Capital being such as to have secured for him the respect and esteem of the members of all parties.

GEO. G. BARTLEY,
(Doorkeeper.)

"Uncle George," as his more intimate friends in the House insist on calling him, was born in Kanawha county, Virginia, November 9th, 1825. In 1829 his father removed to Missouri, and settled in Callaway county when that locality was comparatively a wilderness. Here the subject of the present sketch was raised on a farm, to which vicinity and vocation he still adheres. On the organization of the Legislature of 1858 he was elected Doorkeeper of the House, in which capacity he also served in the Democratic Convention of 1860. He was elected a delegate from his county to the Convention of 1864, and took a prominent part in the proceedings of that body, and on the organization of the present House was the almost unanimous choice of his party for the position he now holds. Though quiet and unassuming, "Uncle George" is always prompt in the discharge of his duties, and is universally esteemed by every one from the Pages up to the Speaker.

T. D. RAPP,
(Official Reporter.)

Mr. Rapp is a native of the Keystone State, where he was born March 17th, 1840. When only four years of age he removed with his parents to Illinois, where his youth and early manhood were spent. Here also he received a thorough education, closing his studies at Rock River University in 1857 as the valedictorian of his class. On leaving school he applied himself to the mastery of the "art preservative," and since has been constantly connected with the press either in the capacity of printer, reporter or editor. He has for the past fourteen years been a resident of St. Louis, during which time he has filled the position of local reporter on the *Press, Dispatch, Times* and *Democrat* of that city. Either as a reporter or writer he is exceedingly rapid and correct. He has discharged the difficult duties of his present position in the House to the entire satisfaction of the body. He also filled the same office in the popular branch of the Twenty-fifth Assembly, which, in view of his avowed political differences with the majority in that body, was the highest compliment that could have been paid to his qualifications.

MEMBERS.

J. D. ABBEE.

Judge Abbee, whose name occurs alphabetically first on the roll of the House, and who represents in the Twenty-sixth General Assembly the county of Polk, was born in Berkshire county, Massachusetts, in the year 1834, and is the only gentleman of Bay-State extraction at present sitting in this wing of the Capitol. But though of Eastern birth, his early removal to and subsequent residence in the West have rendered him essentially Western in sympathy and sentiment, as well as in manners. Before he had reached his ninth year his parents immigrated to Illinois, settling in Boon county in that State. Here the remainder of his youth was spent and the rudiments of his education received, which was subsequently completed at the university at Beloit, Wisconsin. On leaving school he applied himself to the study of the law, and had prepared himself for admission to the bar when the late war breaking out he enlisted in the 95th regiment Illinois infantry, in which he served with distinction for four years, rising from a private to the rank of captain. Returning home on the restoration of peace he was admitted to the bar, and in the following year removed to Polk county, in this State, where he has since resided, applying himself to the practice of his profession. In 1868 he was elected judge of the probate court of his adopted county, a position he resigned in the fall of 1870 to take his seat in the present General Assembly. In politics, Judge Abbee is a Republican of the liberal school. As a legislator, he is attentive and prudent, and although seldom on the floor, is a logical and effective debater. He has proven a most serviceable member of the committees on Constitutional Amendments, Township Organization and Local Bills.

HENRY ABBINGTON.

Who, with Mr. Edwards, represents the populous county of St. Charles, is a native of the Old Dominion, having first seen the light in Henry county of that commonwealth in the year 1808. Leaving his native State to seek his fortune in the growing West he located in 1832 in the county which he at present represents, and where he has since constantly resided. Securing at the outset the confidence and respect of those with whom he was associated in his new home, his subsequent career has been such as to retain for him their good opinions, and has resulted in his frequent preferment to office. After serving as a justice of the peace for a period of nearly twenty years, he was elected in the fall of 1859 to represent his county in the popular branch of the Assembly, a position he held until unseated by the action of the Convention of 1861. Being again elected to the same office in the fall of 1870, he has served his constituency in the present Assembly with marked fidelity, and while one of the oldest members of the body, has been an active and earnest participant in its deliberations. Though an old line Whig in politics, he has under the new order of things allied himself with the Democracy, and been a conscientious and consistent member of that party. On the organization of the House he was assigned the chairmanship of the committee on Justices of the Peace, a position which he has proven himself especially qualified to fill.

J. T. ADAMS.

Dr. Adams, the capable and wide-awake representative from Butler, was born in Humphrey county, Tennessee, January 17th, 1827, where the first nineteen years of his life were spent on his father's farm. Leaving the parental roof in 1846, he removed to Stewart county in his native State, where finding no other means of livelihood open to him, he engaged in wood-chopping, an occupation he continued to follow, until by the strictest economy, he had accumulated means sufficient to enable him to attend the medical school at Nashville, from which institution he graduated with honors in the spring of 1853. The scene of his early labors has since became historic ground, the identical field he assisted in clearing being that upon which the battle of Fort Donaldson was fought in the late war. After completing his studies he applied himself to the practice of his profession in his native county, where he remained until the spring of 1859, when he removed to Missouri, locating in Butler county. Here he continued his practice up to the fall of 1866, when accepting the Democratic nomination for the Legislature he was elected to that office, though subsequently ousted to give place to his Radical opponent. Being re-elected to the same position in the fall of 1868, he was in this instance permitted to take his seat, and served with credit through the Twenty-fifth, as he has also through the Twenty-sixth Assembly. Seldom absent either from the hall or the committee room he has proven a faithful guardian of the interests of his county and the State. His commanding figure and pleasant countenance render him one of the most conspicuous members on the Democratic side of the chamber. He is an efficient member of the Committee on Ways and Means.

P. M. ADAMS,

Who represents the county of Gentry, was born in Clark county, Indiana, in 1841, received his academic education in Montgomery county in that State, and completed his sophmore year at Hanover College in 1862. Abandoning for a time his studies, he enlisted in June, 1862, in the 55th Indiana regiment of three months volunteers, and with that command participated in the exciting chase after Gen. John Morgan, when that cavalier ventured with his command north of the Ohio river. On being mustered out of service in the fall of that year, he resumed his studies at Ann Arbor, Michigan, where he remained up to the summer of 1863, when he again enlisted for a term of six months in the 115th Indiana regiment. Leaving the service again, he devoted his attention to school teaching, and in connection therewith commenced the study of the law. Removing from his native State to Missouri in 1865, he first located in Nodaway, and afterwards in Gentry county, where he has since constantly resided. Being admitted to the bar in 1869, he has since that time applied himself to the practice of law, in connection with his former avocation of school teaching. Receiving the Liberal Republican nomination for Representative in the present Assembly, he was elected to that office in the fall of 1870, and has proven a valuable member of the body. Though rarely a participant in its discussions, he is an attentive and intelligent observer of all that passes in the hall, and ever watchful of the interests of his constituency. He has rendered valuable service as a member of the Committee on the Penitentiary, at whose meetings he is invariably present.

M. S. ALSUP.

Mr. Alsup, who, like the gentleman from Gentry, is among the quiet, though none the less serviceable members of the House, is a native Missourian, having been born in Greene county on the 18th of September, 1836. Removing in 1867 from Greene to Howell, he has since been a resident of the latter county, with whose interests he has become thoroughly identified. On the murder of sheriff Cordell, in 1868, he was appointed by Gov. McClurg to succeed that unfortunate officer, and in the following year was elected by his party in the county to the same position. Identifying himself with the Liberal Republican cause in the canvass of 1870, he received the nomination, which resulted in his election to the seat he occupies in the present House, and which he has filled with unobtrusive ability. No member has been more punctual in attendance, or a more earnest participant in the deliberations of the body.

H. A. APPLEGATE.

The member from Dunklin is a native of New Jersey, in which State he was born December 28th, 1828. Removing with his father to Henry county, Tennessee, in 1839, he was educated and resided there up to 1858, when coming to Missouri he settled in Dunklin county, of which locality he has since been a constant resident. Though raised a farmer, he has about equally divided his time between that calling and merchandising. His first political preferment was in 1866, in the fall of which year he was elected to represent his county in the Twenty-third Assembly. Having secured the confidence of his constituency by the faithful discharge of the duties imposed on him in this instance, he was re-elected to the Twenty-fourth, and again elected to the seat he occupies in the Twenty-sixth Assembly. Though an old line Whig, so long as that party was in existence, he has in later years acted with the Democracy, at whose hands he has received frequent and deserved recognition. On the organization of the House he was assigned to the Committee on Roads and Highways, of which, during the greater part of the adjourned session, he has served as chairman.

J. M. ASHER,

Representative from Clark, was born in Hancock county, Illinois, on the 6th day of April, 1840. During his infancy his father removed to Missouri, locating in Adair county, but after a short sojourn here changed his residence to Keokuk, Iowa, where the youth of the present Representative was mainly spent. Leaving home at the age of nineteen, he returned to Missouri, settling in Schuyler county, where he devoted his attention to teaching school, and commenced the study of the law. When about ready to apply for admission to the profession he had chosen, the late war broke out, and being of stronger Union proclivities than most of those by whom he was surrounded, he abandoned the field of his labors, and going into Kansas enlisted in the 6th Cavalry regiment from that State, in which he served to the close of the war. While in the service, he was several times wounded in action, the honorable scars of which he still bears. On the restoration of peace, he returned again to Missouri, locating in Clark county, where he has since made his home. He was elected in the fall of 1870 as a McClurg Republican to a seat in the popular branch of the Twenty-sixth Assembly, and has taken an active part in the deliberations of that body. A ready and fluent speaker, he has participated in the discussion of many of the more important subjects of legislation, and has done equally valuable service as a member of the Committee on Federal Relations.

ANDREW AUER,

The young and energetic Representative of the Second district of St. Louis was born in that city November 22d, 1842, of German parents. After receiving a thorough business education, first in the public schools and afterwards in one of the commercial colleges of the city, he applied himself to the avocation of book-keeping, which he continued to follow up to 1865, when he commenced the study of the law, reading for a short time in the office of Messrs. Curtis & Moore, and afterwards with his present colleague in the House, Col. N. C. Claiborne. Being admitted to the St. Louis bar in 1868, he has since devoted his time to the practice of his profession in that city. In the fall of that year he received the Democratic nomination for Representative of his district in the Twenty-fifth Assembly, and in the following spring was nominated again by his friends for aldermanic honors, in both of which instances, however, he was unsuccessful. Receiving a second nomination for a seat in the House in the fall of 1870, he was elected by a handsome majority, and since his advent at the Capital has fully demonstrated his fitness for the place. Together with his labors on the floor of the chamber he has proven an efficient member of the Committees on Criminal Jurisprudence, Permanent Seat of Government, Enrolled Bills, and the special committee of the St. Louis Delegation.

W. H. BALLARD,

The popular member who, with Speaker Wilson, represents the county of Platte, was born in Madison county, Kentucky, January 25th, 1835, and educated at Richmond, in that State. Removing to Missouri in the winter of 1859, he located in Platte county, where he has since constantly resided, and with whose interests he has become fully identified. A farmer by avocation, and with no wish or ambition to abandon the quiet independence of that calling for the seductive uncertainties of political life, he has neither sought or held any public place except the seat he fills in the present Assembly. But while comparatively a novice in legislation at the inception of the session, few members more readily comprehended the duties devolving upon them, or have discharged the same with more scrupulous regard for the wishes and best interests of their constituency. Though rarely a participant in the discussions of the body he is a close and intelligent observer, and generally entertains positive opinions on all subjects of importance. On the organization of the House he was assigned by his colleague a place on the committees on County Boundaries, Justices of the Peace and the Blind Asylum, the duties growing out of which he has faithfully performed. Politically, Mr. Ballard is a Democrat of the strictest school.

J. B. BARNES.

This gentleman, in whom the county of Reynolds has found a faithful Representative in the popular branch of the present Legislature, is a native Missourian, having been born at Pilot Knob in what is now Iron county, January 1st, 1837. In the following year his father removed from Iron into what is now Reynolds county. Here the youth of the present member was spent on a farm. Upon attaining his majority however, he abandoned farming and applied himself to the trade of blacksmithing, which he continued to follow up to 1866. In the fall of that year he was elected sheriff of Reynolds county, an office to which he was re-elected in the fall of 1868. On the expiration of the second term of his sheriffalty he accepted the nomination for Representative of his county in the Assembly, a position to which he was elected in the fall of 1870. His course as a member of the House has been marked by close attention to the duties devolving on him both during session hours and in the committee room. Although a Democrat politically, he is scarcely more popular personally with his party friends than with those with whom he most widely differs. He has proven a valuable member of the Committee on Revised and Unfinished Business.

J. W. BARRETT.

Either in his personal intercourse with his associates or on the floor of the House, there is no member more respected or in the fullest acceptation of the word, more popular than the clear-headed, good natured, and at the same time dignified chairman of the Committee on Accounts. The peculiarity of the position he fills renders it necessary that he should know, and be known to everybody, from the Pages up to the Speaker. His bold and characteristic chirography is a *sine qua non* on the warrants on the treasury, and his name is equally respected in that department and in the House. Mr. Barrett is a native of Pennsylvania, having been born in Luzerne county, in that State, in 1822. Enjoying the opportunities of common school and academic instruction in early life, he subsequently, by his own unaided efforts, acquired a thorough collegiate education, graduating at Dickinson college, in his native State. Having completed his studies, he continued to devote his attention to the subject of education, and from 1854 to 1856 was superintendent of public schools in Lycoming county, one of the wealthiest and most intelligent communities in the Keystone State. At the same time he also turned his attention to journalism, and successfully conducted for a number of years the *Independent Press* at Williamsport. Subsequently emigrating westward, he located in St. Louis, where he remained two years, when he removed to Canton, to take charge of the Seminary at that place. Here he established the Canton *Press* in 1862, which he has successfully conducted up to the present time. Mr. Barrett is among the most prominent members of the I. O. O. F. in the State, having been elected Grand Master of the Grand Lodge in 1868, and a representative of the order in the State in the Grand Lodge of the United States in 1869. In addition to his other honors, Mr. Barrett was also elected the first President of the State Editorial association, presiding at its regular sessions in 1868–69–70. He holds his present seat in the House as the Representative from the flourishing county of Lewis, by the wish of his constituency expressed in a majority of 542 votes. Besides holding the responsible chairmanship of the Committee on Accounts, he is also a hard-working and faithful member of the Committees on Printing, Education and Benevolent and Scientific Institutions. Physically speaking, Mr. Barrett is the heavy man of the body to which he belongs, and could probably lift the beam at a weight of 250 pounds.

J. L. BASS.

There are few better looking, and certainly no better members on the Democratic side of the hall, than the estimable gentleman who, with Judge Newman, represents the old and populous county of Boone. Mr. Bass is a native Missourian, having been born October 20th, 1837, in the county whose interests are entrusted to his charge in the popular branch of the present Assembly. Since at the Capital his record has been that of a quiet and laborious member. Though entertaining decided opinions on all subjects of importance to his immediate constituency or the State at large, he has seldom trespassed on the time of the House, and never, I believe, inflicted on the body a set speech. An independent, well-to-do farmer, he has never aspired to or held any office except his present seat, a fact I conceive to be attributable rather to a naturally unobtrusive disposition than any lack of regard or appreciation on the part of his constituency. Besides his labors during session hours, he has served efficiently as a member of the important Committees on the Insane and Deaf and Dumb Asylums and the Committee on Agriculture.

N. M. BELL,

The young gentleman who represents the Fifth district of St. Louis is also a native Missourian, having been born in Lincoln county, November 2d, 1842. After completing his studies in the schools of his native county he removed to the metropolis, where he devoted his attention to mercantile pursuits up to 1864. In the spring of that year he crossed the plains to the Pacific seaboard, encountering on the journey numerous hazardous adventures with the Indians. In one engagement near the famous Horseshoe Bend eight out of eleven of his companions were massacred and he barely escaped under cover of the darkness of the night. After spending several months in the mines of Idaho he visited California, Oregon, Nevada and subsequently Mexico and South America. Returning to Oregon in 1867, he was sent as a delegate from that State to the National Democratic Convention which assembled in New York in the following year. Shortly after this returning to St. Louis, he engaged actively in the grain trade in that city, to which he continued to devote his attention up to the fall of 1870, when he was elected as the Democratic candidate of the Fifth representative district to the seat he has creditably filled in the present House. Few among the younger members of the body have taken a more active part in its deliberations. Mr. Bell is a member of the Committees on Internal Improvements, Lunatic Asylum, Local Bills and the special committee of the St. Louis Delegation.

A. F. BELTRAMI,

Who, as his appearance not less than his name would indicate, is of French extraction and a native of the old French town of Ste. Genevieve, in which he was born December 9th, 1843. With the exception of a short interval in the years 1865 and '66, during which he was engaged in mining in Colorado, he has been a constant resident of his native city and the county he now represents in the lower House. Though his occupation is and has been that of a merchant, he has at times filled various subordinate positions in the offices of sheriff and circuit clerk of his county. By this means he has become thoroughly acquainted with the wants and interests of his constituency which, as their Representative, he has proven himself ever ready to promote. In personal appearance he is perhaps the handsomest member of the Southeastern delegation. He is a member of the responsible Committee on Accounts.

W. H. BENNETT,

Who represented the county of Perry in the Twenty-fifth and has been returned by his constituency to the Twenty-sixth Assembly, is a native of Alabama, having been born in Madison county, in that State, January 9th, 1837. His parents, who were exceedingly poor, removed from Alabama a few months after his birth, locating first at Nashville, Tennessee, and subsequently in Jackson county, Illinois. In the latter locality the present Representative was kept at work on his father's farm until he had reached his fifteenth year, when his parents, pulling up stakes again, removed to Missouri. After visiting various counties in the Southeastern portion of the State, they finally located in Stoddard county where young Bennett again went to work on a farm. After remaining here a few months and having reached his nineteenth year, he left his home and without a cent in his pocket started out in the world to seek his fortune. Making his way to Cape Girardeau he sought and found employment first as a wood-chopper and afterwards as a teamster. After a brief sojourn here he removed to Perry county, where he went to work as a farm hand, an occupation he continued to follow until by strict economy he had accumulated means sufficient to enable him to attend school. After attending school for a short period he applied himself to school teaching in connection with the study of the law, and in 1867 had made sufficient progress in his studies to enable him to graduate from the law department of McKendree College, Illinois. In the mean time he had also taken part in the civil war, entering and continuing in the Federal service as long as his conservative sentiments would permit him to do so. Since graduating he has devoted himself to the practice of his profession in Perry county. Mr. Bennett is essentially a self-made man. As a legislator he is laborious, clear-headed and conscientious, and as a speaker, fluent, forcible and continuous. Politically he is a life-long Democrat. He has proven a valuable member of the Committees on Criminal Jurisprudence, Elections and Enrolled Bills.

JOHN L. BITTINGER.

Mr. Bittinger occupies a seat in the Legislature this winter as the successor of the present State Treasurer, Samuel Hays, from the First representative district of Buchanan county, embracing the greater portion of the flourishing city of St. Joseph. A Pennsylvania Dutchman, in which State and condition he was born in 1833, Major Bittinger is still essentially Western in all his instincts, as he is also in his manners. Emigrating from his native State, he located in St. Louis in 1855, and after a residence of five years in that city, removed still further westward, locating at St. Joseph, where, with the exception of short intervals, he has since resided. In 1861 he was appointed postmaster at St. Joseph, and which he was up to 1865. A practical printer by early education, he is among those who have worked their way from the "case" into the "sanctum." Since the establishment of the St. Joseph *Herald*, in 1862, he has been the editorial head of that vigorous Radical sheet, and, with C. B. Wilkerson, has contributed largely to the success and prosperity the enterprise has achieved as the mouth-piece of the party in the Northwest. Major Bittinger is by no means a novice in legislation, having served his present constituency in the Twenty-second Assembly, of which he was Speaker *pro tem.*, and his return gives evidence of the confidence imposed in his integrity and ability. During the war he was aid-de-camp to Governor Willard P. Hall, in which position he rendered efficient service to that officer. He was also a member of the commission appointed by the Secretary of War in 1862 to assess damages sustained by "loyal" sufferers by the war, which commission, it will be remembered, was afterward dissolved without results. Connected with the press in one capacity or another from boyhood up, Mr. Bittinger has occupied numerous positions of honor and responsibility, and to his thorough knowledge of his business in all its intricacies is mainly due the success of the *Herald*. A man of energy and resource, he is, perhaps, capable of more hard work, either of head or hand, than any member on the Radical side of the House. He is an admitted shrewd manager, and measures to which he has devoted himself in his party have seldom failed of success. As a speaker, he is always brief, sententious and pointed, and without pretention to oratory, he is nevertheless effective and always conspicuous and convincing. Of about the average stature, he is of robust, and yet compact build, with an open expression and unusually intelligent countenance, and by the most casual observer would be taken for what he is—one of the leading members on the Radical side of the chamber. Mr. Bittinger is chairman of the important Committees on Internal Improvements and Insurance, and also a member of the Committees on Retrenchment and Reform, on Printing and Congressional Apportionment.

J. H. BOHN.

The jocose and good natured Representative from Benton county, is also a native of the Keystone State, in Franklin county, of which commonwealth, he first saw the light in the "Ides of March," 1826. In 1832 his father removed with his family to Stark county, Ohio, where the present Representative, to use his own language, commenced his collegiate course in a log school house. Shortly after this, on losing his mother, he returned to the place of his birth, and thence made his way to Baltimore, where he placed himself under the care and tuition of his father's brother, a gentleman of the highest moral character and great piety. Remaining here but a short time, however, he left his relative's roof, the cause of difference between them, again to employ his own language, being, that while his pious preceptor strove to direct his efforts toward the pulpit, his own inclination and special qualifications pointed in the direction of the stage. After leaving Baltimore, he oscillated for a number of years between the States of Pennsylvania, Illinois, and Ohio, finally bringing up in Springfield, in the last named State, in 1859, where in the office of the Hon. Samuel Shellabarger, he commenced the study of law. After completing his studies and being admitted to the bar, he returned to Illinois, where, at the first call for troops for the late war, he entered the 92d Illinois regiment, in which he served as a Major until the restoration of peace. On leaving the service he settled in Benton county, in this State, where he became engaged in lead mining, and where he at present holds the position of superintendent of the Pioneer Mining and Smelting Company. In 1866 he was elected public administrator of his adopted county, and in 1868 was elected to a seat in the lower house of the General Assembly, a position to which he was re-elected in the fall of 1870. Politically he was an old line Whig, though his course in Missouri has been that of a Republican of the liberal school. In his personal associations at the capital he has rendered himself universally popular, and as the original "Little Brown Jug," will be long remembered after his seat shall have been filled by a more sedate member.

WILLIAM BOSBYSHELL.

No member of the present Assembly more thoroughly represents the practical, common sense, working class than Mr. Bosbyshell, of the Eighth representative district of St. Louis. Economy and practical legislation are his strong hobbies. Seldom or never absent from his post, he invariably records his vote in strict accordance with his ideas of what is right and proper. Mr. Bosbyshell is a native of Pennsylvania, having been born in the Quaker city in 1827. At the early age of thirteen he emigrated to the West, where he has since been engaged in active pursuits, and by strict attention to business, indefatigable energy and unswerving integrity, has amassed a handsome fortune. During his time his life has been an eventful one, he having followed, with success, at least a dozen avocations. Commencing as a raftsman he shortly rose to the captaincy of a Missouri river packet. Afterwards a merchant, he is now one of the largest livery men and stock dealers in the West. Serving four years in the city council of St. Louis, he has acquired a reputation for honesty and devotion to principle which has made him invincible as a candidate for any office of trust or emolument, despite the Radical majority he has had to contend against in his ward. Since his advent at the State capital he has made hosts of friends, by whom his judgment on all matters is regarded as sound and dictated purely by integrity of purpose. His constituency have occasion to feel proud of him, and his record will be an indorsement of their good judgment in sending him to the seat he so worthily occupies. Mr. Bosbyshell, like the worthy chairman of the Committee of Accounts, of which he is also a member, is among the weighty men of the House. He is the possessor of a robust physique, a full, good natured and intelligent countenance and an ease of manner which renders him at home in any and all situations. Though seldom indulging in long speeches he frequently puts in a word in the right place.

W. A. BRADSHAW.

The venerable member from Miller county, is a native of Kentucky and was born in Adair county, in that State, June 8th, 1817, where he followed the life of a farmer up to 1859, when he removed to Missouri, settling in the county whose interests have been intrusted to his charge in the present Assembly. On the outbreak of the war, taking a decided stand in favor of the unity of the States, he raised a company of militia with whom he repaired to the State Capital, where he remained until his command was disbanded. Returning home he was elected a judge of the county court, a position he continued to hold until 1870, when elected to represent his county in the House. Though rarely on the floor, he is seldom out of his seat, and is invariably attentive and assiduous in the discharge of the duties imposed on him. Like Mr. Bosbyshell, he is among the weighty members of the body. Politically, he is a Republican. On the organization, he was assigned to the Committee on Enrolled Bills, of which he has proven a capable member.

J. J. C. BREAZEALE,

Who represents the county of Christian, is a Tennesseean, in which State he was born December 4th, 1833. On attaining his majority he immigrated to Missouri, locating first in Newton and afterwards in Christian county, where he has since constantly resided, and with whose interests he has made himself fully acquainted. It has been his good fortune in his new home to have had various positions of honor and emolument assigned him—having held nearly every office in the gift of his constituency from that of constable up to Representative. He was sheriff of his adopted county for two terms from 1866 to 1870, finally refusing renomination to accept his present position in the House. His course at the Capital has been marked by strict attention to and a faithful discharge of the duties imposed upon him. Politically Mr. Breazeale is a Republican, and by calling a farmer. He is a member of the Committee on Immigration.

LUMAN A. BROWN.

The authorship of the important bill for the equalization of the assessment and collection of the tax on railroads, would in itself, perhaps, stamp the member from Howard county as one of the most practical, clear-headed and eminently serviceable members of the House. Seldom out of his seat during session hours, and seldom, if ever, absent from committee meetings, where his presence is desired, and his experience and judgment are often called into requisition, I know of no member more strictly faithful to the interests of his immediate constituency or the State at large, nor one more conscientious in the discharge of the duties imposed upon him. Having said this much, I am gratified at being able to add that Mr. Brown is a Democrat without a thought or shadow of turning. A native of Connecticut, from which State he emigrated to Missouri in 1857, he is an exemplification of the staunch Democracy of the wooden nutmeg State. On removing to the West Mr. Brown located in Howard county, where he has since resided, universally respected and esteemed for his estimable qualities of heart as well as head, and by whose people he has been twice chosen to represent them at the State Capital. Though the present House may be regarded as one of young men, it is hardly necessary to remark to those who know him that the member from Howard, though approaching sixty, is in no respect an old fogy or lacking the spirit and vigor of the youngest of his co-laborers. With these qualities he combines an experience and maturity of judgment which causes him to be frequently consulted, and at all times respected by his younger associates. In personal appearance Mr. Brown is rather under the average hight, with an expressive, and at all times pleasant countenance, a fine forehead, quick eye and sprightly, nervous manner. Though often upon the floor, and especially when matters in which he is particularly interested are under consideration, he is never tiresome, but at all times listened to with respect and attention, and seldom fails to carry his points. This, however, it should be added, is owing rather to the subject matter than the manner of what he has to say, as he makes no strain at oratory, and seldom betrays either feeling or passion in his delivery. Mr. Brown is an active, I might say, invaluable member of the Committees on Ways and Means, Internal Improvements, Agriculture, Penitentiary, Blind Asylum, County Boundaries and the special committee to investigate the affairs of the Normal Schools in the First and Second districts.

MILTON C. BROWN.

Few counties are better represented in the House than the populous and thoroughly Democratic county of Monroe, in the person of its young, energetic and wide-awake member, Mr. Milton C. Brown. A native of Mississippi, and a descendant of one of the oldest and best families of that State, he possesses all the fire and impetuosity of the Southern temperament, united with a good judgment and sagacity that seldom, if ever, permit him to blunder. Emigrating at an early period from his native State, Mr. Brown located in Illinois, from which State he entered the Federal army as a private, at the breaking out of the war, and remained in the service until the war was perverted from a struggle for the unity of the States into a crusade against the liberties and property of the South, when he sought and obtained an honorable discharge. Returning to civil life, he devoted his attention to the study of the law, and in the meantime removed to this State, locating in Monroe county. Here he completed his studies, and was licensed to practice by Chief Justice Wagner. In connection with the practice of his profession, he also turned his attention to journalism, and in 1868 established the Monroe City *Appeal*, a live, progressive and 'red hot" Democratic journal, which he conducted with signal ability and success. Representing, as he does, one of the first agricultural and stock growing counties of the State, it has been his province during the session to devote a large share of his attention to these interests as affected by legislation. Mr. Brown is also the author of the admirable bill introduced early in the session regulating passenger tariffs on railroads, and a similar measure regulating the shipment of stock. Generally punctual in attendance, and seldom absent from his seat during session hours, his name will be found recorded among the ayes and noes on every important measure that has yet been brought to the attention of the House. He is chairman of the Committee on Local Bills, and an active member of the Committees on Internal Improvements.

R. BUCKHAM,

Representing the northwestern county of Atchison, is one of the older members of the House, having been born in Sumner county, Tennessee, June 25th, 1811. During his infancy his family removed to Kentucky, where his youth and early manhood were spent, and where he graduated in medicine, a profession he has since continued to follow. Immigrating to Missouri in 1836, he located first in Boone and subsequently in Atchison county, where he has since constantly resided. He was elected a member of the Twenty-third Assembly and returned by his constituency to the present House, in which he has proven a faithful and efficient guardian of the interests of his county and the State at large. Though he has seldom occupied the floor, he is not without his opinions on subjects of legislation, which, when expressed, invariably command the attention and respect of his associates. He has been a serviceable member of the important Committee on Ways and Means. Politically he is a Republican.

LUZERNE L. BULKLEY.

The capable and conscientious Representative from Ralls is a native of Indiana, in which State he was born May 25th, 1837, and where he remained until six years of age, when his family removed to Missouri, settling in the county of Ralls, where they have ever since resided. After receiving a good common school education he commenced farming, an occupation his father had followed before him, and to which he continued to devote his attention until the late war broke out, when at the first call he entered the service and served with the rank of Captain first in the 2d and afterwards in the 11th Missouri regiment. On the restoration of peace, turning his spear into a pruning-hook and his sword into a plowshare, he returned home and again engaged in farming, which peaceful avocation he continued to follow up to the fall of 1866, when he was elected to a seat in the Twenty-fourth Assembly. The experience he gained in this body he has turned to excellent account in the present House, and has enabled him to prove a most valuable member. Politically Mr. Bulkley is a Liberal Republican. He has served efficiently as a member of the Committee on Banks and Corporations and the special committee on Fees and Salaries.

R. F. BULLER.

The flourishing county of Cedar, which has given the State its Lieutenant Governor, has done itself equal credit in sending to the other chamber of the Capital the present occupant of desk No. 53. Mr. Buller, though among the younger members of the House, had already acquired a reputation in his profession at home, which, preceding him to Jefferson City, secured for him early in the session a position on the Committee on the Judiciary, a position which he has since abundantly proven his fitness to hold, and one in which he has done most excellent service. No member of the committee, I venture to say, aside from Mr. Thomas, its most efficient chairman, has taken a more active part in its deliberations, or exercised a more positive influence upon its decisions. A shrewd and well read lawyer, fully acquainted with the present statutes, and knowing their defects, he has assiduously applied himself, with his associates on the committee, to the work of amendment and modification demanded of the present Assembly. Having positive views upon most subjects, he has seldom failed to express them on the floor of the House with independence and candor, and never, I am confident, failed to vote as his conscientious convictions have dictated. Nor has his disposition in this regard in any instance been restrained by party considerations. Whenever he has had occasion to differ in opinion from the majority of his Democratic associates, he has invariably, and without hesitation, done so. Though lacking in some respects the ease and grace of the orator, his remarks upon all subject are thoughtful, logical, and put with a terseness and vigor of expression which renders them generally effective. He is a frequent participant in the debates of the House, though never tiresome or needlessly wordy. Mr. Buller is in his thirty-first year, and a native of Canada West. Since his fourteenth year he has been a resident of the United States, having at different periods resided in New York, Iowa and Missouri. In stature he is slightly above the medium hight, of fine figure and possessing an intelligent and pleasant countenance. All in all, few counties are better represented in the present House than the county of Cedar.

S. W. BUNCH.

The Democratic Representative of Taney first saw the light January 19th, 1831, in Simpson county, Kentucky, where he resided up to 1840, in the spring of which year his family removed to Missouri. Since leaving his native State he has resided at different times in Iowa and Northern Missouri, finally bringing up in Taney county, where he was elected to and held the office of assessor for the years 1855-6-7-8 and 1859. On leaving this office he engaged in the occupation of farming, taking no part in politics up to the fall of 1870, when he was elected to the seat which he at present holds in the House. His record since at the Capital has been that of a quiet worker, seldom out of his seat and always casting his vote in accordance with his conscientious convictions of duty. No county has had a more faithful guardian of its interests. He was placed by the Speaker on the Committee on County Boundaries and Engrossed Bills, on both of which he has done excellent service.

JOSEPH H. BURROWS.

Who represents the county of Mercer was born near the city of Manchester, England, May 15th, 1840, and is the only gentleman of British birth sitting in the House. When he was only two years old his parents emigrated to the United States, landing at New Orleans, where his mother died the following year. After this bereavement his father removed first to Quincy, Illinois, and thence to Keokuk, Iowa, where he also died of cholera in 1840. The present Representative after his father's death, was left in charge of his uncle, at whose hands he received the advantage of a common school education, and on leaving school he adopted a mercantile life, which he has since continued to follow. Removing to Missouri in 1861, he located first in Putnam, then in Harrison and finally in Mercer county. Even before leaving Iowa he entered the political arena and espoused the cause of the Little Giant in the memorable contest of 1860

Since in Missouri he has been a consistent member of the Republican party, at whose hands he holds his present seat. Mr. Burrows is likewise a minister of the Baptist denomination, and in 1867 united with his other labors also that of editing the Mercer County *Advance*, his county newspaper, which he continued to conduct through the canvass of that year. As a legislator he has applied himself assiduously to the discharge of the duties devolving on him both during session hours and as a member of the Committee on Claims.

J. G. BURTON.

The worthy member from Randolph claims the distinction of being the fattest member of the House. He is a native of Virginia, having been born in Orange county in that State in the year 1812, which renders him also one of the oldest members of the body. While he was only an infant his parents removed to Kentucky, and after a sojourn of several years in that State, again removed to Missouri, settling in Randolph county in 1840. Here the present Representative has since constantly resided, securing the esteem of all who know him, and receiving at their hands repeated preferment to positions of honor and trust. He was chosen to represent his county in the Twenty-fifth Assembly, and re-elected to the present body in the fall of 1870. Though seldom consuming the time of the House in speech-making, he is nevertheless a hard-working and influential member, and a gentleman of clear comprehension and the most unimpeachable honesty. Politically, he is a Democrat of the strictest school, and by occupation a farmer. He has served during his present term as a member of the Committee on Engrossed Bills.

F. C. BUTLER,

Who, like the gentleman from Randolph, is one of the older members of the House, was born in what is now the county of New Madrid, March 10th, 1805, where, with the exception of short intervals, he has ever since resided. He has at different times followed various avocations and been honored with frequent elevation to office by his constituency, his political career commencing in fact at a date anterior to the birth of many of his younger associates in the present Assembly. His first office was

CYRUS H. FROST.

SPEAKER PRO TEM.

that of constable, to which he was elected in 1832. Having filled this position for two years, he was elected sheriff, and served in this capacity for two terms. In 1842 he was again elected sheriff; in 1844, chosen to represent his county in the Legislature, and in 1850 elected judge of the county court, which latter position he continued to hold until ousted by the memorable ordinance of 1865. His election to the present House will probably be the last of many official trusts imposed upon him by his constituency, his already extreme age and feeble health having prevented him from taking as active a part in the legislation of the session as his inclination and regard for the interests of his county and the State would have induced him to have done. Though politically an uncompromising Democrat, he is equally popular with the members of all parties, and has won the esteem of every one with whom he has been associated at the Capital.

G. F. CHILTON,

Representing the county of Shannon, was born in Monroe county, Tennessee, in 1836. When five years of age his father removed with his family to Missouri, locating in Shannon county, where the present Representative was raised and has ever since resided, devoting himself to agriculture and stock-raising. In his nineteenth year he became deputy county and circuit clerk, and in 1858 was appointed deputy sheriff, serving as such until 1860, when he was elected sheriff of his county. In 1866 he was appointed and in 1868 again elected to the same responsible office, and as a still higher mark of the good-will and esteem of his fellow citizens he was in 1870 chosen to represent them in the Legislature. In politics he is a sound Democrat, and as a man and a legislator he has won the confidence and respect of his associates. Quiet and unostentatious in his deportment, and making no pretentions to oratory, he yet is a working member, a close observer and always votes with judgment. He is a member of the Committee on Library and the special committee to revise the Revenue law.

N. C. CLAIBORNE.

Col. Claiborne, representing the Sixth district of St. Louis, was born in Franklin county, of the Old Dominion, February 15th, 1822. His ancestry settled in the colony of Virginia in the early part of the seventeenth century. His father, Hon. N. H. Claiborne, was for a long term of years in Congress, and his uncle, Hon. Wm. C. C. Claiborne, the first governor of Louisiana. After receiving a liberal education, Col. Claiborne chose the profession of the law, which he has continued to follow through life. His first preferment to office was in 1847, when he was elected a member of the Virginia House of Delegates, in which he served up to 1851, when he was chosen a delegate to the Constitutional Convention of his native State which met in that year. In 1857 he removed to Missouri, locating in Kansas City, where he soon acquired a reputation and large practice at the bar. He was chosen by his party in his new home a delegate to the National Democratic Convention of 1860, in which he stood by the Little Giant to the last. In the fall of the same year he was also elected a member of the House of Representatives from Jackson county, a position which in the following year he resigned to remove to St. Louis and engage in the practice of his profession in that city. He was Secretary of the Senate during the called session of 1861, and has since been twice elected to the House from St. Louis. Such is a brief sketch of his distinguished career. Of his eccentric genius, brilliant accomplishments and rich, genial, hearty humor it is difficult to speak with justice. "Nat Claiborne," as his thousand friends insist on calling him, not only wins all hearts, but he carries them by storm. His humor, his flashing, pointed, but never envenomed wit, his boundless generosity, his uniform kindness of heart render him always and everywhere a delightful companion. Though a zealous and uncompromising Democrat, he is personally the friend and favorite of all parties. As a parliamentary orator it is safe to say that he has not an equal in the House.

R. A. CLARK.

The capable member from Dade county was born in Gettysburg, Pennsylvania, in 1822, where he remained until fourteen years of age, at which time his father immigrated with his family to the West, locating in what is now Benton county, in this State, when that locality was comparatively a wilderness. Here the present Representative remained, working on his father's farm up to 1849, when being seized with the gold fever, which at that date swept over the country, he set out for California with the first immigration to that State. After an eventful sojourn of two years on the Pacific slope, he returned to Missouri, and in 1851 located at Melville, in Dade county, where he has since continued to reside. During the administration of Mr. Lincoln he was appointed postmaster of that village, an office he has ever since filled. His present seat in the House is the first and only position he has held by the suffrages of his fellow citizens, but though a novice in legislation on his arrival at the Capital, he has fully acquainted himself with the responsible duties devolving on him, and has proven an efficient and faithful Representative of the interests of his county. Politically Mr. Clark is a Republican, and his present avocation is that of a merchant. He is a valuable member of the Committee on Mines and Mining.

GEO. B. CLARK,

Representative from Washington county, is especially known in the House as the first among the soldiers of the "lost cause" to occupy a seat in either branch of the General Assembly. Major Clark was born May 8th, 1833, in Hallowell, Maine. Having enjoyed peculiarly favorable educational advantages during his boyhood, he had, at the age of twelve, completed his preparatory studies for a collegiate course, when all his plans were changed by the death of his father, and he found at once devolved upon him, in a great measure, the care and support of his mother, and four children younger than himself. Entering with alacrity upon the struggle with destiny thus opened before him, he employed himself successfully, during the two following years, in occupations not especially adapted to the advancement of his tastes and ambitions. By this time he had so far mastered stern necessity as to enable him to seek such more congenial occupation as might be open to him, and he entered the law and school book printing establishment of Masters, Smith & Co., in his native city, as an apprentice. Having spent four years in that office in the acquirement of "the art preservative," he at once removed to the South, locating in Georgia. There, for several years, he was more or less prominently connected with the daily press of Savannah and Augusta in various capacities, and subsequently with the Atlanta *Republican*. In 1857 he set out upon a tour of several of the Atlantic seaboard and Northern cities, employing himself in the meantime at his trade. In 1858 he reached the West—the aim of his trip—and settled in Missouri. In St. Lous he at once found profitable employment at the printing business, and pursued it until able to complete a course of law study previously undertaken. At the end of a year's study, he was licensed as an attorney before the St. Louis circuit court, and within a month thereafter removed to Potosi, the county seat of Washington county, where he has since resided. In June, 1861, he espoused the cause of the South, and served in the Confederate army until the surrender of the last forces in the field, in June, 1865. After this event he spent a short time in Louisiana and Texas, thence going to Mexico. During the reign of the unfortunate Emperor Maximilian, he divided his time between agricultural enterprises and the establishment and conduct of a semi-weekly newspaper, printed in both the English and Spanish languages, at Orizaba, Mexico, entitled "The Railway *Era*." In the fall of 1866 he returned to Missouri, and was connected with "The *Hesperian*," a literary production of St. Louis, during its brief existence. In April, 1867, he resumed his residence at Potosi, and established the "Washington County *Journal*," which now holds rank as a leading Democratic newspaper in Southeast Missouri, and with which he still retains his connection. Re-enfranchised only upon the submission of that question to the popular vote in 1870, he refrained from taking any part in political affairs until that date. In the spring of 1871 the seat of Representative from Washington county in the General Assembly becoming vacant by the death of Hon. J. P. B. Gratiot, he received the Democratic nomination of his county to the position, and at a special election held in August last, was elected by a highly complimentary majority, In the adjourned session of the Assembly, he has been an active member of the important standing Committees on Internal Improvements and Federal Relations, as also upon the special committees appointed to investigate the claims of the 81st and 82d regiments E. M. M., and the joint committee for the purpose of reporting a uniform system of common pleas and probate courts. As a speaker, Maj. Clark is fluent, logical and impressive, and never fails to secure and retain the attention of the House when on the floor. Personally, he is scarcely less popular among those who differ most widely with him than among those of his own political faith.

W. F. CLOUD.

One of the shrewdest, clearest-headed and most influential members on the Republican side of the chamber is the gentleman upon whom it has devolved to represent the county of Jasper in the present Assembly. Col. Cloud was born in Champaign county, Ohio, March 23d, 1825, his parents having removed to that State from Virginia and Maryland. His education was only such as was afforded him in the common schools of his native State, and this had scarcely been completed when he enlisted and served through the Mexican war as an Ohio volunteer. On quitting the service, he returned home and shortly afterwards removed to Kansas, where he resided up to the outbreak of the late struggle between the States, when on the 21st of April, 1861, he offered the first company for service to the Governor of that State. His services being accepted he was, on the organization of the 2d Kansas, elected and commissioned a Major in that regiment. After the battle of Wilson's Creek, he was promoted to a colonelcy, with which rank he served gallantly to the close of the war, always in command either of a regiment, a brigade, or a district. On the restoration of peace, he returned to his home in Kansas where he remained up to 1867, when he removed to Missouri locating in Jasper county, where he has since been engaged in the real estate business in connection with the practice of law. Though holding firmly to the tenets of the Republican party, he is tolerant of the views of his opponents, and among those who believe that the exigencies of the late war and the results that have followed, have developed in those who espoused the cause of the South a degree of patriotism and devotion to principle that entitle them to all the immunities of citizenship, and that general amnesty at this time would prove advantageous to the country. Col. Cloud is a member of the Committees on Deaf and Dumb and Lunatic Asylums, on which he has done valuable service, together with his labors during session hours.

J. P. COLCORD.

The Representative from the Seventh district of St. Louis, who, with Nat Claiborne and the member from Mississippi county, furnishes the pyrotechnics of the House, is a native of Suckerdom, having been born in Bond county, in that State, in 1843. Graduating with honors at the reputable institution at Greenville, in his native county, in 1861, he entered the Federal army during the following year, and served creditably up to the spring of 1863, when he was severely wounded while leading his command to the attack on Vicksburg. Retiring to civil life he located in St. Louis in 1864, where shortly afterwards he commenced the practice of law. About the same time he was also associated with Judge Fogg, late of the Supreme bench, as Secretary of the commission to revise the General Statutes of the State. In 1866 he was appointed prosecuting attorney of St. Louis county, and at the fall election in that year was elected by the people to the same office for the term of four years. In the triangular contest in the fall of 1870 he was elected to the seat he now occupies in the House over his Democratic and McClurg opponents. Politically, Mr. Colcord is a Republican of the most liberal school, seldom, if ever, hesitating to take issue with his party associates when his convictions lead him to differ with them. He took a conspicuous part in the memorable bolting convention, and stumped St. Louis and other counties for the Liberal ticket. Besides his professional and official duties, Mr. Colcord has been an almost constant contributor to the press, and will be remembered as the author of the "Sketches of the St. Louis bar," published in one of the city dailies. In his intercourse with his associates, Mr. Colcord is universally courteous and popular. As a speaker, he is ready, fluent and inexhaustible. He is frequently on the floor, and generally speaks with point and effectiveness. He is of slender build, nervous and active in all his movements, and glories like a woman in a long luxuriant growth of hair, which is brushed Byronically back of his ears. He is a serviceable member of the Committee on Criminal Jurisprudence, and has also served on various special committees.

F. N. COLEMAN,

Who represents the county of Carter, is a native of Tennessee, having been born in Polk county, in that State, December 5th, 1834. Removing to Missouri in 1851 he located, and has since constantly resided in the county which he represents in the present Assembly. Though an unpretentious farmer and never having sought political preferment, he has twice been honored with office at the hands of his constituency, first in being elected public administrator of his county and subsequently in being chosen a member of the lower branch of the Legislature. Politically, he is an uncompromising Democrat. His course since his advent at the Capital has been marked by close attention to the business of the House and a faithful discharge of the duties immediately devolving upon him. He is a member of the Committee on Claims.

S. C. COLLIER,

Representing the rich mineral county of Madison, is the "rough diamond" of the House. Unpretentious, reserved, absolutely silent in fact for weeks at a time, he is perhaps the last gentleman in the hall who would be picked out for an orator, much less *the* orator, if I may make a single exception, of the body. His extreme modesty and taciturnity render him one of those whom you are slow to become acquainted with. You get at the rich kernel only through a thick shell, but how rich it is you can only know when you have penetrated the shell. You find him genial, warm-hearted, earnest and true. With a large fund of information he combines a clear and logical discrimination and a compact and felicitous diction. His eloquence is of the purest quality. Its groundwork is a terse and luminous statement of facts on which is built a solid superstructure of logic. There runs through his discourse a rich vein of poetic imagery and sentiment which charms and magnetizes the listener, while his unanswerable arguments carry with them conviction. His speech during the regular session on the question of calling a Constitutional Convention will sustain all that I have said regarding his oratory. Mr. Collier was born in the county which he at present represents in the House, October 19th, 1825, and was educated at Cumberland University, Lebanon, Tennessee. He studied law in the office of the Hon. Samuel Caruthers, and since his admission to the bar has followed that profession as a means of livelihood. He was an active member of the Constitutional Convention of 1861, to which he was elected by a larger majority than that given any other delegate to the body. Politically he is a Democrat of the strictest school. He is a member of the important Committee on Mines and Mining and the Commtttee on Justices of the Peace.

M. CROCKETT,

Representative from Andrew, was born in Seneca county, Ohio, January 11th, 1825. In 1857 he removed to Missouri, settling in Andrew county, where he has since made his home and with whose interests he has become thoroughly acquainted and identified. On the outbreak of the war he entered the Federal service, and continued therein until peace was restored, serving first as a private and afterwards as a lieutenant. The only office he has ever held prior to his election as a member of the present House, was that of postmaster of his native village under the administration of President Pierce. Mr. Crockett is by calling a farmer, and politically a Republican of the liberal school. As a legislator he is attentive, industrious and conscientious, generally in his seat and casting his vote with good judgment. He is a member of the Committee on Claims, from whose meetings he is seldom absent.

DANIEL E. DAVIS.

The Southwest has sent no more serviceable a member to the present Assembly than the shrewd, good-natured and intelligent Representative from Pulaski county. Invariably punctual in attendance, and closely attentive to the business of the House, it can be said of Mr. Davis what can be said of few of his associates, that he has been present at every meeting and adjournment of the body, and has as yet failed in no instance to answer to his name at roll call. Always voting, he has also voted with invariable intelligence and a conscientious regard for the best interests of his constituency and the people at large. With a decided vein of humor in his composition, it has frequently devolved upon him to arouse the House from its stupors and restore cheerfulness and good nature. Mr. Davis is a native of the county he represents, where he was born in 1835. Having emigrated with his father when quite young to California, his early manhood was spent upon the Pacific slope. Returning to Pulaski county in 1861, he enlisted and served with credit for one year in the Federal army as a captain in the Forty-eighth regiment Missouri volunteers. In civil life Mr. Davis has at various times followed the calling of farmer, mechanic and merchant, in all of which he has applied with success the tact and energy for which he is distinguished. In politics he is a Democrat of the strictest type, always acting in harmony with his party associates in the House. He has proven an efficient member of the Committees on Library and on Benevolent and Scientific Institutions.

JOSHUA DEAN.

No member on the Democratic side of the chamber has by his conscientious course at the Capital achieved a more untarnished reputation for honesty and regard for the over-burthened tax-payer than the worthy member from DeKalb. Though making no effort at oratory, he never fails to raise his voice against extravagance in any shape, and has in every instance proven a friend of retrenchment and reform. Mr. Dean is a native Missourian, having been born in Jackson county, in this State, April 12th, 1832. He has resided for a number of years in the county which he at present represents in the popular branch of the Assembly with whose interests he has become thoroughly identified. A quiet and unpretentious farmer by calling, he has never sought or held any public office prior to the seat he now holds in the House. He is a member of the Committee on Roads and Highways.

EPHRAIM DENT,

Who represents the county of Hickory, is also to the manor born, having first seen the light in Franklin county, in this State, December 12th, 1831. During his boyhood his family removed to Polk county, where they resided for five years, at the expiration of which period they removed to St. Clair county. After a sojourn of nine years in the latter locality, the present Representative removed to the county of Hickory, where he has ever since resided. In 1862 he was appointed by Gov. Gamble to fill a vacancy on the bench of the county court of his adopted county, and in 1866 was elected to the office of county assessor, which latter position he filled for two years. He was elected in the fall of 1870 as an independent Republican to the seat which he at present holds in the House, and which he has filled with ability and a scrupulous regard to the interests of his county and the State. On the organization of the body he was assigned to the Committee on Engrossed Bills.

J. S. DOAK.

The affable, kind-hearted and clear-headed gentleman who represents the county of Crawford, is among the older members of the House, having been born in Augusta county, Virginia, in 1808. Removing to Missouri in 1830, he has since that date been a resident of this State, and the greater portion of the time of the county whose interests have been placed in his charge in the present Assembly. He has followed by turns the callings of farmer and merchant, and is at present engaged in the former pursuit. As a legislator he has been attentive, laborious and faithful. Politically a Democrat, he has proven true to his party and its principles in all questions of a political character, while personally he has won for himself the respect and esteem of his associates irrespective of party. He has served on the important Committees on Education, Mines and Mining and Permanent Seat of Government.

ALBERT G. DOD.

Who represents the county of Knox, is a Kentuckian, having been born in Danville in 1841. His father was for many years professor of mathematics in Centre College, in that State. The present Representative received a thorough classical education, graduating with honors from the Illinois College at Jacksonville, and on completing his studies entered the Federal service in the late war, in which he served up to the restoration of peace. On leaving the service he settled in Knox county, in this State, and engaged in farming and stock raising, which pursuits he still continues to follow. In the exciting political canvass of 1870, he ran as an independent Republican for the seat he at present fills, and was elected by a majority that fully attested his personal popularity among his friends. Although one of the younger members of the House, he has proven a cool-headed, as well as an active participant in its deliberations, and gives promise of great future usefulness to his constituency. He has been the author of a number of important measures of a general character, and has served as chairman of the Committee on Revised and Unfinished Business, and as a member of the Committee on Agriculture. He was also selected by the Speaker from among the young men of the House as a member of the committee to receive the Grand Duke Alexis on his recent visit to the Capitol.

J. H. DOLLE.

The member from Bollinger was born February 22d, 1822, and is a native of Germany. In 1836 he immigrated to the United States, and about one year thereafter settled in Missouri. Up to 1868 he had refrained entirely from taking any active part in politics, preferring to give his undivided attention to his private pursuits—farming and milling—but in the fall of that year being solicited by his friends to emerge from his retirement, he accepted the nomination for Representative from his county in the General Assembly, and was elected by a highly complimentary majority. The acceptability of his services in this instance secured for him a renomination and a re-election to the present House, in which his course has been one of continued devotion to the interests of his constituency. Though rarely on the floor, he is equally as rarely out of his seat, and seldom, if ever, errs in his judgment or his vote. Though a Republican, he never permits politics to interfere with his duties as a legislator. He has rendered good service as a member of the Committee on Justices of the Peace.

P. R. DOLMAN.

The gentleman on whom it has devolved to represent the populous and intelligent county of Chariton in the present House, is a native of Ohio, in which State he was born in 1836. When only nine years of age he removed with his father to Missouri, settling first in St. Louis and subsequently in Chariton county, in which latter locality he has, with the exception of short intervals, continued since to reside. Having first received a thorough academic education, he commenced the study of the law, and for that purpose entered the office of Col. A. S. Harris, with whom he continued to read, up to the outbreak of the late war. In the summer of 1861 receiving an order from Gen. Fremont to raise troops in his county, he laid aside his books and at once entered upon the discharge of that duty, and as an acknowledgment of his services, received a Captain's commission in the 18th regiment Missouri volunteers on the organization of that command. After active field service in the early Western campaigns, he was taken prisoner at the battle of Shiloh, and made the rounds of the Southern prisons. Being exchanged, he rejoined his regiment in Mississippi, and shortly afterwards was assigned to provost marshal duty at Chewalla, Tennessee. Being promoted to the rank of Major in 1864, he served with General Sherman in his march on Atlanta, up to November in that year, when he was mustered out of service. On leaving his command he returned to Chariton county, where finding a reign of terror, he, at the solicitation of his fellow-citizens, took command of the county, and straightway succeeded in restoring peace and order. In the same year he was promoted to the rank of Colonel in the State service. Since the war he has devoted his time to the practice of his profession. He has twice been the nominee of his party for the seat he at present occupies, having been defeated in 1868 by Judge Salisbury, his Democratic opponent. His course since at the Capital has given ample attestation of his fitness for the place. He has taken an active and intelligent part in the consideration of all subjects of importance, and done valuable service as a member of the Committees on Militia and County Boundaries.

D. A. EDENS,

With the single exception, possibly, of the gentleman from the Sixth district of St. Louis, there is no member on either side of the chamber who possesses in a greater degree the gift of natural oratory than the sprightly and intelligent Representative of the rich agricultural county of Mississippi. Few have engaged more freely in the debates of the session or done so with less apparent effort or preparation. Mr. Edens is a native of Kentucky, having been born in Graves county, in that State, October 26th, 1837. Removing with his father to Paducah in 1850, he completed his education in the schools of that city, and immediately thereafter commenced the study of the law in the office of Governor J. Q. A. King. On being admitted to the bar in 1860, he removed to Missouri, and settled in the flourishing village of Charleston, where, with the exception of three years spent in the South during the war, he has since continued to reside. His superior talent as an advocate gave him at once the first rank at the bar in his new home, and have secured for him a large and lucrative practice. In the fall of 1870, he accepted at the hands of the Democracy of his county the nomination which resulted in his election to the seat he occupies in the present House. As a Representative he has, aside from his active participation in matters of general legislation, been a watchful and conscientious guardian of the interests of his immediate constituency, whose claims to consideration he has never failed to present. Though politically a red-hot Democrat, his personal intercourse with his associates has been such as to have made for him friends in all parties. He is a member of the Committees on Militia and Swamp Lands.

A. H. EDWARDS.

Among the younger members on the Democratic side of the House, no one has wasted less of that legislative time, which some one has estimeted to be worth $7 a minute, than the intelligent, though reserved and modest occupant of desk No. 21, who, with Mr. Abbington, represents the flourishing county of St. Charles. While in no sense of the word inattentive or indifferent to the business of the House, Mr. Edwards has almost entirely abstained from taking part in the oftentimes frivolous discussion of minor questions, though in the few speeches he has made on the leading measures of the session, he has shown that he is by no means wanting in opinions or the power to express them. A lawyer of good attainments and varied experience, and possessing in an unusual degree "the rare quality of common sense," he is a valuable and laborious member of the important Committees on Criminal Jurisprudence, Enrolled Bills, the Pententiary and Printing, upon whose deliberations he exercises a positive influence. Mr. Edwards is a native of the Old Dominion, having first seen the light in Henry county, in that State, in 1836, which, by a singular coincidence was also the native county of his colleague. His parents moved to St. Charles county in 1838, where he has acquired a good education and fairly entered upon the battle of life, and where, for so young a man, he has held prominent and responsible positions. Mr. Edwards is a gentleman a little above the average hight, of erect and graceful carriage. His thoughtful face would at once arrest the attention of the most casual observer.

A. C. EUBANKS,

The member from Sullivan, was born in Pike county, Ohio, June 16th, 1832. In 1837 his father removed with his family to Missouri, locating in Audrain county, where the youth and early manhood of the present Representative were spent, and where he continued to reside up to 1861. On the outbreak of the late war, taking a decided stand in favor of the unity of the States, he enlisted in the 2d regiment of Missouri cavalry, and served as a lieutenant in that command up to 1864. On leaving the service in the spring of that year, the war then being practically over, he located in Sullivan county, where he has since continued to make his home, and at the hands of whose people he has received frequent preferment to office. In 1866 he was elected prosecuting attorney of his county, and in the same year chosen a Representative in the popular branch of the Twenty-fourth General Assembly. His experience in that body has rendered him one of the most serviceable members of the present House. Though a lawyer of superior attainments and good practice, Mr. Eubanks is essentially a self-made man, his only educational advantages, when a boy, having been those of the log-school-house days. As a legislator he is industrious, prudent and practical, and as a speaker ready, terse and logical. Politically, he is a Republican of the liberal type. Besides his labors during session hours he has done efficient service as a member of the Committee on Criminal Jurisprudence.

JOHN F. FASSEN,

Representing the Carondelet district of St. Louis county, is a Hollander, having been born in the city of Utrecht, September 12th, 1836, where the first thirteen years of his life were spent and the rudiments of his education received. In 1849 he immigrated to the United States, and located in St. Louis county, Missouri, where he has since continued to reside. Though a farmer by calling, he has for a number of years taken an active part in politics, and been honored with frequent preferment to office. In 1866 he was elected a justice of the peace of Carondelet township; in 1868 chosen to represent his district in the popular branch of the Twenty-fifth Assembly, and in 1870 re-elected to a seat in the present House. His experience of four years at the Capital has given him a thorough knowledge of the routine of legislation and the intricacies of the rules, and renders him entirely at home in his seat. Though rarely trespassing on the time of the body, he never fails to raise his voice in favor of any measure redounding to the interests of his immediate constituency. Politically, Mr. Fassen is a Republican. He has served as a member of the Committees on Permanent Seat of Government and Benevolent and Scientific Institutions, and the special committee of the St. Louis Delegation.

JOHN L. GANZHORN.

A more thoroughly practical member probably does not sit in either wing of the Capitol than the worthy gentleman recently elected to fill the vacancy occasioned in the Second district of St. Louis by the death of Mr. Borg. Though only a few weeks in his seat, it may be remarked that he is already fully up in the business of the House, and has become thoroughly accustomed to the legislative harness. Mr. Ganzhorn is a native of Pennsylvania, having been born in the Quaker City, January 26th, 1832, but for the past fourteen years has been a resident of St. Louis, and closely identified with the business interests of that city, which he thoroughly comprehends and especially represents on the floor of the present House. During the late war he was an extensive contractor with the general government, and since that time has held the same relation to the city government of St. Louis, in both of which he has acquired a reputation for business tact and energy united with the strictest integrity. For the past four years he has also held the position of school director in his district, and is at present chairman of the township board of education for St. Louis township. Since a member of the House he has been always at his post, attentive, laborious and faithful in the discharge of his duties, and as a recognition of his eminent practical qualifications he has been assigned by the Speaker to the important Committees on Internal Improvements and Ways and Means.

GEO. W. GATES,

Representing the eastern district of the populous county of Jackson, is a native of Vermont, in which State he was born in 1807. After receiving a thorough academic education he applied himself to the study of the law, and had about prepared himself for admission to the practice of that profession, when circumstances compelling him to change his plans, he turned his attention to mercantile pursuits, which he continued to follow up to within a few years past. His private affairs, however, have by no means prevented him from filling numerous positions of public trust, and probably no one of his associates in the present House can exhibit an official record more varied or extending over a longer period of time. While a resident of the East he was for a number of years sheriff of his native county, a postmaster under Jackson and Van Buren, and United States Marshal of the Eastern district of Vermont under the latter President. Suffering a heavy loss by fire in 1849, he sought to recover his fortune in the West, and with that view emigrated to Illinois where he sojourned up to 1865, when he removed to Missouri, locating in Jackson county. Here he was elected a justice of the county court in 1866, and to the seat he at present occupies in the House in 1870. Politically, Judge Gates is a Democrat of the old school. As a legislator he takes an active and intelligent part in the proceedings of the body of which he is a member, entertaining decided views on all subjects of importance, and never failing to express them. He has proven a serviceable member of the Committees on Internal Improvements and Roads and Highways, besides acting as chairman of the Committee on the Penitentiary.

IRA F. GEORGE,

The Representative from Camden, is a native of the Old Dominion, having been born in that commonwealth in 1816. When twelve years of age he emigrated with his father to the neighboring State of Kentucky, where his early life was spent, and where he continued to reside up to 1850, when he removed to Missouri locating in Miller county, where he served for two years as a judge of the county court. In 1858 he removed to Camden county his present home, where he filled the offices of justice of the peace and county court justice almost constantly up to the fall of 1870, when he was elected to his seat in the present House. Politically, Mr. George is a Liberal Republican, and his course, in all instances, has been in strict accordance with the principles of that party. Born of poor parents and denied even the advantages of a common school education, he has nevertheless by close observation, aided by natural good sense, in a large measure overcome his early misfortunes. Though personally modest and taciturn, amounting almost to reticence, he is still not lacking in amiability and social virtues. The good people of Camden might have chosen a gentleman as their Representative of more brilliant accomplishments, but one more faithful to their interests, or of greater probity and sterling worth, it would be difficult for them to find.

MICHAEL GIRDNER.

The estimable gentleman sitting in the present House as Representative from Barton county, is a Kentuckian, having been born in that commonwealth in 1814. After spending the first twenty years of his life in his native State, he removed to Missouri, locating in Barton county, where he has since continued to make his home. By calling, Mr. Girdner is a farmer, which pursuit he has followed since a boy, abandoning it for the first time in the fall of 1870, to accept his present seat in the House, the only public office he has ever aspired to or filled. Though a novice in legislation, however, his county could not have sent a more faithful Representative of her interests to the State Capitol, or one more assiduous and conscientious in the discharge of his duties. Politically, he is a life-long Democrat, and has acted in harmony with his party associates on all questions of a political character. He is a serviceable member of the Committee on Revised and Unfinished Business.

J. E. GOODSON.

The populous county of Macon has found an efficient and zealous guardian of her interests in the worthy gentleman whose name heads the present sketch. Dr. Goodson, though a Kentuckian by birth, removed at an early age to Missouri, and has since been a constant resident of the northeastern portion of the State, the peculiar interests and wants of whose people he fully comprehends. Before locating in Macon, his present home, he was for a number of years a resident of Carroll, from which county he was elected to the lower branch of the General Assembly nearly twenty years ago. The experience gained in that body he has fully availed himself of in the present House, and few members are apparently more at home in the legislative *role*. Though past his fiftieth year, he is quite as active a participant in the business of the body as the youngest of its members. Accustomed, as a minister of the Gospel, to public speaking, he is always at ease on the floor, and never fails to command the attention of the body. He has been the author of a number of the most important bills that have passed this session, and has done faithful service as chairman of the Committee on the Blind Asylum, and as a member of various special committees. Politically, the doctor is an uncompromising Democrat.

EDMUND GRAY.

There are few brighter or more intelligent faces on the Democratic side of the chamber than that of the capable, though modest, in fact almost reticent member from Scott county. Captain Gray, as his more intimate friends address him, is a native of Ohio, having been born in Cincinnati, August 20th, 1834. When a lad of fifteen he removed to St. Louis, in which city he continued to make his home up to 1854, when he removed to Gray's Point, his present residence in Scott county. Though now engaged in farming, he has up to within a few years past followed the responsible calling of a pilot on the Ohio and Mississippi rivers. The first and only office he has ever held on shore is his seat in the present House. Since at the Capital his course has been such as to secure for him the respect and esteem of his associates, and the confidence and satisfaction of his constituency. Politically, he is a Democrat of the strictest school, He has served as a member of the Committee on Accounts and on several of the special committees.

JNO. B. HAAS,

The member from Moniteau, is, as his name would indicate, of German origin, having been born in the city of Loudan, in the Bavarian Palatinate, in the year 1832. In 1846 his father emigrated with his family to America and settled in St. Louis, where the subject of the present sketch was employed as a clerk in a mercantile house until 1853, when becoming weary of the monotony of that life, and under the impulse of an attack of "gold fever," he started to California and crossed the plains as an ox-teamster. Arriving at Salt Lake, he spent the winter with the Mormons, and in the spring continued his Western journey in charge of a cattle train, and after much hardship and many narrow escapes, arrived at Sacramento City. Here he became an accomplished Californian of that era, following by turns the callings of miner, wood-chopper, newspaper correspondent, hotel keeper and justice of the peace, besides at one time owning a large sheep ranche. He also took the first pack-train of merchandise across the Sierra Nevada mountains to Gold Hill, when the mining excitement first broke out in that vicinity. Having seen enough of wild life in the gold regions, in 1866 he returned to St. Louis, and soon afterwards removed to Moniteau county, where he now resides. Politically, he is a Republican of the liberal school. His course in the House has been such as to win for him the highest regard and esteem of his fellow members. He has served as a member of the Committees on Federal Relations and Local Bills.

F. HACKMAN,

Representing the county of Warren, was born in the kingdom of Hanover in 1824. In 1835 his parents immigrated to the United States, settling in Warren county, where they have since continued to reside, and where the present Representative was raised on a farm. Since attaining his majority he has still adhered to agricultural pursuits, abandoning that quiet and independent life for the first time to accept the seat to which he was elected in the General Assembly in the fall of 1870. Though a Republican, he is still a gentleman of liberal and conservative views, and in no instance has permitted partisanship to interfere with his duties as a legislator. Seldom absent from his seat, he is a close observer of all that transpires in the chamber, and invariably votes as his judgment and conscience dictate. He is a member of the Committee on Manufactures, from whose meetings he is seldom absent.

N. C. HARDIN.

On the Democratic side of the chamber and among the younger members of the House, it would be difficult to select one who reflects greater credit upon either than the estimable gentleman who, with his senior in years, Judge Murray, represents the populous and prosperous county of Pike. Though a novice in legislation at the inception of the session, he brought to his aid a superior scholastic and legal education, combined with a naturally quick perception which soon enabled him to acquire a thorough acquaintance with the business of the House in which he has participated throughout his stay at the Capital, with intelligence and an invariable regard for the best interests of his constituency and the people at large. Deferring, however, to those of longer experience he has seldom indulged in the discussion of merely technical questions, and has seldom, if ever, therefore wasted any of the time of the session. Still, while this is the case, he has by no means been a silent member. His speech in advocacy of the proposition for a Constitutional Convention, delivered early in the regular session, secured for him a reputation as a debater which his record since has fully sustained. Rarely absent from the chamber and always attentive to pending measures, his vote is invariably cast as his judgment dictates and the public interest requires. Mr. Hardin is a native Missourian, having been born in the county which it has devolved on him to represent in the present Assembly, in 1846. Having received a thorough academic and collegiate education, he applied himself to the study of the law, and graduated with distinction from the famous Harvard law-school at Cambridge. On being admitted to the practice, he was almost immediately elected city attorney of Louisiana, Pike county, a position held in their earlier professional days by John B. Henderson, Geo. W. Anderson, Judge Fagg and others of that distinguished bar. When intrusted with the responsible duties of this office he had hardly attained his majority. He is still successfully engaged in the practice of his profession in his native county. Of about the average hight, of robust physique, a broad and well-rounded chest, and a good natured and engaging countenance, he may be classed among the best-looking as well as among the most intelligent members of the House. As an acknowledgment of his superior qualifications he was assigned by the Speaker on the organization of the body to the important Committees on the Judiciary and Internal Improvements.

M. B. W. HARMON,

The member from Nodaway, is a native of the Keystone State, having first seen the light in York county, of that commonwealth, March 26th, 1836. When fourteen years of age he removed to Ohio, where he resided for five years, when he removed to Illinois. After a residence of two years in Suckerdom he again pulled up stakes and made his way to Georgia, where he engaged in the book trade. On the outbreak of the late war he left the South and returning to Ohio, enlisted as a private in the 31st regiment of infantry from that State, in which he served in every capacity from private up to colonel commanding. During the war he also served for a time on the staff of Gen. Thomas and other general officers, and participated in all the more important engagements of the West, being several times severely wounded. Having served gallantly through the war, on the restoration of peace he removed to Missouri, locating in Nodaway, of which county he has ever since been a resident. A good soldier, he has also proven a good citizen, and succeeded in securing the entire confidence and esteem of those with whom he has been associated in his new home. As a mark of their good opinions he was chosen by a highly complimentary majority to the seat he occupies in the present House, the duties growing out of which he has faithfully and conscientiously discharged. Politically, Mr. Harmon is a Republican of the liberal school. He has been an efficient member of the Committees on Manufactures, Township Organization and the special committee on the Revenue.

W. R. HARRIS,

The member from Montgomery, was born in Albemarle county, in the Old Dominion, December 31st, 1812. On completing his education he engaged in the occupation of school teaching, which he continued to follow for five years and until his removal from that State. In 1837 his father immigrated with his family to Missouri, locating in Montgomery county, where he was joined by the present Representative in the following year. On his arrival in his new home he again applied himself to school teaching which he again followed for twelve years. In 1850 he was elected to the office of justice of the county court of his adopted county, and at the expiration of his term was re-elected to the same position. In 1858 he was chosen by a highly complimentary vote to represent his county in the popular branch of the General Assembly, and in 1860 was re-elected to the same office, holding his seat until ousted by the memorable ordinance of the Convention of the following year. Since that date he has resided in private retirement on his farm near Montgomery City, emerging into public life for the first time in 1871 to accept the seat in the present House rendered vacant by the death of the Representative from his county. Though a recent arrival at the Capital, he is by no means a novice in legislation, but has throughout the adjourned session taken an active and intelligent part in the deliberations of the body. Politically, he is a Democrat, and personally, a gentleman of the old school.

W. L. HICKMAN.

The member from the Thirteenth district of the county of St. Louis was born in Winchester, Kentucky, December 19th, 1822, and is therefore fifty years of age. During his infancy his parents removed to Missouri settling in St. Louis, where his youth was spent and his education received. On completing his studies he removed into the country and engaged in farming, which occupation he has, with the exception of short intervals, since continued to follow. In company with a party of fortune-seekers, he crossed the plains to California in 1853, but after a sojourn of one year in the gold regions, returned home. He also made a trip with another party to Pike's Peak in 1859, but after a brief stay in that locality, again returned to his family and his farm in St. Louis county. On the outbreak of the late war receiving the appointment of enrolling officer of his district, he entered the service and continued therein up to the restoration of peace, filling various offices and posts of honor, in all of which he acquitted himself with great personal credit. Espousing the cause of Liberalism in the canvass of 1870, he was elected by his party to the seat which he at present fills in the House. Of a naturally quiet and retiring disposition he has seldom occupied the floor in the discussion of less important measures, though his course has been marked by close attention to the business of the body, and an intelligent consideration of all subjects effecting the welfare of his immediate constituency and the State at large. He has been a valuable member of the Committees on Claims and on Agriculture.

D. S. HOOPER,

Representing the county of Adair, was born in Perry county, Ohio, in 1825, and is the son of a clergymen, who served as a Captain in the American army in the war of 1812. After receiving a thorough academic and collegiate education he continued to reside in his native State up to 1857, when he emigrated to Missouri and settled in Adair county. Upon the outbreak of the late war, taking a decided stand as a Union man, he assisted in raising the first company of volunteers which was organized in his county, and declining any office as a reward for his services, enlisted as a private soldier. In September 1861, however, he was promoted to a Lieutenancy and assigned to duty as Post Quartermaster at Macon city. In 1862 his regiment having been consolidated with another he was mustered out of service, but again commissioned as Lieutanant in the fall of 1862, and placed upon recruiting service, and upon the formation of the 27th Missouri Infantry regiment, was commissioned as Captain. He was finally discharged from service on account of physical disability in 1864, and appointed clerk of the Adair county circuit court, serving as such until 1867, when he was appointed sole judge of the county and probate courts of the same county. In the political campaign of 1870, he was the candidate of the regular Republican party of his county for the position he now holds, and was elected over his opponent by a handsome majority. Since at the Capital he has proven a valuable hard-working member of the House. A close and accurate reasoner, and a fluent speaker, he supports his views upon all matters under discussion with ability and zeal, and has the credit of introducing and ably advocating several of the most important measures of the session. He is a member of the Committees on Retrenchment and Reform, and also the Committee on Printing.

THOS. J. HOWELL,

Is one of the veteran Democrats of the body, this being the sixth time that he has represented the county of Oregon in the lower House of the General Assembly. He was born in Smith county, Tennessee, in 1808, where he also was raised and educated. In 1835 he removed to Kentucky, from which State in 1740 he moved to his present residence in Oregon county, when that county formed a part of Ripley. He was one of the first judges of the county court of Oregon, and his first term in the Legislature was in 1842. Though a farmer by occupation, and naturally possessing but few of the requisites commonly supposed to be necessary to constitute a succesful politician, has probably been associated with the political history of the State longer and more intimately than any member of the present House. The frequent calls made upon him by his own people to serve them as their Representative, exhibits an appreciation of his character, that his pure life and sterling probity fully warrant. The county of Howell was named in his honor. In the present Assembly he has served as a member of the Committees on Manufactures and Revised and Unfinished Business.

GEO. H. HUBBELL.

A more intelligent and conscientious legislator or more polished and affable gentleman can scarcely be found on either side of the chamber, than the worthy Representative of the county of Grundy. Mr. Hubbell was born in St. Lawrence county, New York, 1818. After completing a course of studies in civil engineering, he was employed professionally in the preliminary survey of the great Erie railroad, and also in Martineau's survey of the celebrated Croton waterworks in his native State. On removing to Missouri in 1835, he was three years a student at Marion College, near Palmyra, and on leaving that institution taught school and studied law in Howard county. He was licensed and admitted to the bar in 1841, and the following year removed to Grundy county, where he has since resided, and been engaged in the practice of his profession. In 1847 he was elected circuit clerk of his adopted county, which office he continued to fill for eighteen consecutive years. In 1870 he was chosen to represent his county in the present House, of which body he has proven a laborious and influential member. Courteous in his manners, moderate in his political opinions, with discriminating judgment, and as a speaker forcible and effective, and possessing the faculty of always impressing his hearers with his own sincerity of purpose, he has taken an active part in shaping the legislation of the session. He has served as a member of the Committees on Federal Relations and Roads and Highways.

THOMAS G. HUTT.

Though the present House is essentially one of young men, it is, however, by no means lacking in that gravity, experience and maturity of judgment, which is looked for and more generally found in those of riper years. Among those whose frosted hair and uniformly dignified deportment give character to the body, no one on the floor or in the less restrained associations of legislative life, enjoys in a greater degree the confidence and respect of all, and especially of his younger associates, than the member from Lincoln county. A native of the Old Dominion, in which glorious commonwealth he was born in 1817, Mr. Hutt is peculiarly a gentleman of the old school, pleasant in address, easy and attractive in manners, possessed of a keen and ready perception, most excellent judgment and a scrupulous regard for the interests of his constituents, he may be described, in much shorter phrase, as an agreeable gentleman, an efficient, laborious and conscientious legislator. Seldom among the absentees, either from the House, or the committee-room, he has discharged the duties that have devolved upon him with uniform fidelity and intelligence. Though a Democrat of the strictest school, he has in no instance betrayed a forgetfulness of that courtesy due those who differ with him; and I am doing him but simple justice, I believe, in saying that he is quite as popular, personally and socially, on the Radical side of the chamber as with his own party friends and associates. Mr. Hutt has been a resident of Missouri and of the county he at present represents for over thirty-four years, during which time he has made himself fully acquainted with their interests. He is at present engaged in farming, although for a series of years he has discharged the duties of the office of clerk of the circuit court of Lincoln county. In personal appearance he is about the average hight, of robust physique, an open, intellectual and pleasant countenance. His hair and whiskers, of which he has a bountiful growth, are almost as white as snow, making him a marked man as he sits at his desk surrounded by younger, but not more efficient or more active members. He has been an efficient member of the Committees on Internal Improvements, Township Organization and County Boundaries.

GEO. W. KITCHEN,

The wide-awake and clear-headed member from Stoddard, was born in Terre Haute, Indiana, November 17th, 1842. During his infancy his family removed to Missouri settling in Stoddard county, of which locality he has since been a constant resident. Since attaining his majority he has at different times followed the avocation of farming, milling and merchandising, in each and all of which he has applied the indomitable energy which constitutes the most conspicuous trait of his character, the result of which has been the accumulation of a handsome fortune. In 1866 he was elected sheriff of his county, and in 1868 was re-elected to the same position. During his second term, it devolved upon him to execute the sentence of death on the notorious Skagg for the murder of General Richardson at Memphis, Tennessee, the circumstances attending which are still fresh in the public mind. Elected in 1870 as a Liberal Republican to the seat he occupies in the present House, his course as a legislator has been marked by the strictest regard for the interests of his constituency, while in his intercourse with his associates both during and out of session hours has been such as to render him universally popular. He has served as a member of the Committees on Justices of the Peace and Swamp Lands.

WILL J. KNOTT.

It is perhaps the misfortune of the majority in the present House that it has not a recognized leader. Among those whose judgment is consulted and whose opinions are deferred to most frequently by their associates no one approximates more nearly to leadership than the clear-headed, conscientious and indefatigable member from Osage county. The general correctness of his views, the untarnished honesty and integrity of his personal character, his insinuating manners, and, withal, his familiarity with the business of the body and the intricacies of the rules, gives him an influence and power which is recognized alike by friend and foe. His advocacy of any measure is little less than a guarantee of its success, while his opposition, which is never the result of prejudice or traceable to personal motives or interest, is almost a certain defeat. While a ready, pointed and fluent speaker, he makes no effort, however, at oratory. In the subject matter, rather than the manner of his delivery, lies the effectiveness of what he has to say. The fact, also, that he never speaks for the mere love or pride of speaking, but only when his convictions of duty impel him to do so, secures for him the invariable attention of the body. Mr. Knott is a native Missourian, having been born in St. Charles county in 1836. He has resided at various times in St. Louis, Callaway and Osage counties, finally settling in the latter county in 1856, in which he has since continued to make his home, and where he is at present engaged in manufacturing. Recognizing his superior qualifications, he was chosen by his present constituency to represent them in the popular branch of the Twenty-fifth Assembly, in which body his legislative experience began. It was during the adjourned session of that Assembly that the important measures looking to the political reinstatement of the disfranchised classes in the State were carried through, and to no one of the minority in that body was their success more attributable than to Mr. Knott. During the same session, also, he rendered invaluable service on the special committee to investigate the management of the Penitentiary, and was in a large measure instrumental in bringing about the much-needed reforms in that institution. Re-elected to the present House, he has labored not more earnestly, though much more effectively, with the majority of this body. Besides his untiring labors during session hours, he has served as chairman of the important special committees on the Revenue, on the Registration law and the committee to investigate the management of the Lexington and St. Louis railroad, and has been a member of the Committees on Printing and the Deaf and Dumb and Lunatic Asylums. Politically, Mr. Knott is a Democrat, and will lose no fair opportunity to strengthen his party in the State. In personal appearance he is rather under the medium hight, with a clear sharp black eye, a fine complexion and a good head, which sets easily, almost jauntily, upon broad, square shoulders and a generally robust physique.

AUGUST KOCH,

Representing the Third district of St. Louis, was born in Westphalia, Prussia, in 1818. He attended the common schools of the country until twelve years old, when, with a view of perfecting himself in the modern languages and natural sciences, he went to a private institution of learning where especial attention was given to those branches of study. After finishing a regular course there, he entered a mercantile establishment to obtain a practical knowledge of commercial pursuits, and remained there until he attained his twentieth year, when, under the inexorable military laws of Prussia, he was compelled to enter the army. After performing one year's service he obtained permission to emigrate and came to America, landing in New Orleans in 1840. He remained in New Orleans and the South, engaged in commercial operations until the Mexican war begun, when he enlisted as a private in the 2d regiment of Louisiana volunteers, and did service on the Rio Grande and under Gen. Taylor until the six months for which he enlisted expired, when he was appointed interpreter of the French and Spanish languages to the chief of subsistence, which position he filled until the close of the war. Removing to Missouri, he lived in the State only one year, and then in 1850 went across the plains to California, suffering all the hardships incident to this journey at that early period in the history of the then unknown West. In 1854 he returned to St. Louis, where he has since resided. Though a gentleman of superior education and possessing a large fund of practical information, he is nevertheless among the more quiet and reserved members of the House, and has taken little or no part in the debates of the session. While this is the case, however, no member is more intelligently observant of the business of the body, or votes on all questions with better judgment. Politically, Mr. Koch is a conscientious and consistent Democrat. He has been a useful member of the Committees on Immigration, Revised and Unfinished Business, and the special committee of the St. Louis Delegation.

D. L. KOST,

The capable member from Daviess, is a native of Ohio, having been born in Knox county, in that State, February 18th, 1835. After receiving a thorough scholastic education he removed to Illinois, and subsequently to Kansas, and after a brief sojourn in these States returned in 1860 to his native State and commenced the study of law in the office of Hon. Mr. Shellabarger at Springfield at the same date that his colleague in the present House, Mr. Bohn, was reading with that gentleman. In the following year he graduated with credit at the Ohio Law School at Cleveland, and was shortly thereafter admitted to the bar of his native county. At the outbreak of the late war between the States he enlisted in the 65th regiment of Ohio infantry, in which he served as a private up to August, 1863, when being honorably discharged, he returned to his home, and a few months thereafter removed to Missouri, locating in Daviess county, of which locality he has since been a constant resident. Here he commenced the publication of the *North Missourian*, a vigorous Republican newspaper, which he continued to conduct up to 1870 in connection with the practice of his profession. In 1868 he was appointed and served as superintendent of registration for the Fourth Senatorial district, and in 1870 was chosen to represent his county in the popular branch of the Twenty-sixth Assembly. Of a naturally superior intellect, cultivated and developed by study, a good writer, and fluent and forcible speaker, he has discharged the duties devolving on him at the Capital with fidelity and marked ability. Besides his valuable services during session hours, he has been an active and influential member of the Committees on Elections and Insurance, and the special committees on Revenue and Common Pleas and Probate Courts.

J. C. LAMSON,

Representing the extreme Southwestern county of McDonald, is a New Yorker, having been born in Jefferson county, in that State, in 1834. In 1837 his father immigrated with his family to Ohio, and after a sojourn of three years in that State removed to Indiana, where the youth of the present Representative was spent, and where he continued to reside up to 1859, when he removed to Missouri, settling in Polk county. After a sojourn of one year in this locality he again pulled up stakes and set out for Texas, and after a brief stay in the Lone-star State visited Minnesota, and thence returned to his old home in Indiana, where he enlisted in the 17th regiment of mounted infantry from that State, which at that time was being organized for the late war. In this command he continued to serve for four years and four months, throughout which period he was constantly in active field service, and participated in all the important engagments of the army of the Tennessee. On leaving the service he paid a second visit to Missouri and located in McDonald county, where he still resides, and with whose interests he is thoroughly identified. Mr. Lamson is a gentleman of superior scholastic and legal education, having graduated before the war at Oberlin, Ohio, and afterwards at the law university at Albany, in his native State. He is at present engaged successfully in the practice of his profession in McDonald and the adjoining counties. Though among the most quiet and unobtrusive members of the House, he is a close observer of all that transpires in the hall, and always votes with intelligence and good judgment. Politically, he is a Republican. By an oversight of the Speaker the only committee to which he was assigned on the organization was that of Local Bills.

J. W. LANGSTON,

Representing the First district of Greene, including the flourishing city of Springfield, is a native of Kentucky, having been born in Logan county, of that commonwealth, October 5th, 1829. When an infant his family immigrated to Southwest Missouri, settling in Greene county, where the present Representative was raised on a farm. Taking a decided stand in favor of the unity of the States in the late war he entered the State service, in which he participated in the battle of Springfield, in which he was taken a prisoner. Since the war he has led the life of a quiet and independent farmer. In the late disruption of the Radical party he espoused the liberal cause, and was elected on that ticket to the seat he occupies in the present House, the duties growing out of which he has conscientiously discharged. He is a member of the Committee on the Library.

HENRY J. LATSHAW.

This gentleman was born in Canada, in 1835, and lived for some time in Illinois, where he entered into a successful business and became prominent as a Democrat in the politics of the State. He removed to Missouri in 1866 and settled in Kansas City, where he engaged extensively in the lumber trade, extending his operations far down into Kansas, Texas, and the Indian Nation. In all the commercial enterprises of his city he took a prominent part, making a specialty of grain shipments, to control which, he built a very large and commodious elevator. In 1870 he was elected as a Democrat from the Western district of Jackson county, to the lower House of the Missouri Legislature. Appointed chairman of the Committee on Ways and Means—one of the most necessary and important in legislation—he entered at once upon his duties with the same business energy and intelligence that had characterized his operations in private life. As a speaker, he is forcible, logical and fluent, relying more upon the solidity of his arguments than upon their adornment, more upon his facts than his rhetoric. In his intercourse with his colleagues, he is polite, accommodating and agreeable, understanding thoroughly the etiquette due in the conflicts and clashings of policies, and knowing how to insist with firmness and yield with good nature. A large experience and much practice have fitted him particularly as a working member of the Legislature. The propositions that come from his hands are always clear and convincing, and no bill is left unfinished until he has mastered it in every point in which it can be presented. His mind is of the analytical kind, seeking rather to satisfy its own doubts first before attempting to remove the doubts of others. This makes him ardent, earnest and enthusiastic, and prevents him from being a luke-warm friend or a kindly enemy. His convictions come from the head and not from the heart, hence, as a legislator, while he is always safe he is sometimes most positive. In the contest of 1870, he took a prominent part, carrying his district handsomely, in spite of a most rigid registration, and was one of the hardest and most consistent workers in the Democratic ranks. The choice of many for the mayor of Kansas City, and, later, for a seat in Congress, he yet waived all aspirations in the peculiar nature of the crisis, preferring rather to give a Democratic Legislature to Missouri than to insist upon withdrawing from a race in which another man would have been beaten.

BENJAMIN LEACH,

Who represents the county of Gasconade, was born in the State of Illinois in 1815, and consequently may be classed among the older members of the House. At that early period in the history of the West when schools were scarce and educational facilities limited, he had the advantages of attending a common school for only about six months. Marrying in 1837, he was ordained a minister of the Baptist church in 1839, and soon thereafter removed to this State, where he has since resided. For many years he has been a warm friend of the free school system, and a laborer in behalf of its promotion. In 1868 he was the Republican candidate to represent his county in the General Assembly, but was defeated, but in the last canvass he was elected as a Liberal to the same position by a highly complimentary majority. He is a quiet, taciturn member, but a gentleman of modest worth and sterling integrity. He has served as a member of the Committee on Manufactures.

W. T. LEEPER,

The member from Wayne, is the unquestioned leader of the retrenchment and reform element in the House. While he cannot be called an orator, he is nevertheless a forcible and effective speaker. His style of thought and expression is strong common sense uttered in equally strong language, wherein lie the elements of his success and influence over the more practical minds of the body. He is among the most attentive and industrious members of the House, and it is safe to say that no measure of general interest has escaped his notice and no attempted extravagance, however well concealed, escaped his scrutiny. Decided in his convictions and fearless in their utterance, he boldly grapples with whatever he deems to be wrong or erroneous. Mr. Leeper was born in Maury county, Tennessee, in 1823, and spent his youth on his father's farm. Removing to Missouri in 1857, he settled in Wayne county, in which locality he has since resided, following the calling of a farmer. He has taken an active part in politics for the past twelve years. He was a member of the memorable convention of 1861, in which he strongly opposed the withdrawal of Missouri from the Union. At the outbreak of the war he entered the Federal service as a Captain, and continued therein up to the restoration of peace. On leaving the service he took the stump in opposition to the adoption of the Constitution of 1865, canvassing the greater portion of the Southwest. He was a member of the Twenty-fifth Assembly, in which, his course as it has been in the present body, was that of a zealous and consistent Democrat. In addition to his valuable services in his seat and on the floor of the House, has been an influential and hard-working member of the Committees on Education, Revenue and County Boundaries, of the latter of which he is chairman. He has also served on several of the most important special committees.

JAMES S. LOGAN,

The Representative from the county of Carroll, was born in Harrison county, Ohio, in 1812. During his infancy, his father taking his family and household goods upon a keel-boat, started down the Ohio river in search of a home in the Western wilds, and settling in Perry county, of this State, opened a farm. After a few years of rough experience, the family moved to Jackson county, Illinois. It was while they were living here that the "Black Hawk" war began, and young Logan, though a mere stripling at the time, enlisted and served to the close as a private soldier. After this he studied medicine in Columbia, Illinois, and subsequently removed to Ralls county, Missouri, where he opened a drug store. In 1843 and 1844 he attended the lectures at Kemper College, St. Louis, in the latter part of 1844 removed to DeWitt, Carroll county, where he has ever since resided, devoting himself exclusively to the practice of his profession, until in the fall of 1870, having received the nomination of the Liberal Republicans for the office he now holds, he made an energetic and successful canvass of the county, and was elected by a decided majority. In politics, Dr. Logan is a bold and outspoken conservative,. who has worked faithfully and efficiently to preserve intact the organization and carry out the principles of the Liberal party. Personally, he is a gentleman of pleasing address, and much sincerity of manners. He has made several lengthy arguments upon the floor of the House on important subjects, and, as a speaker, is noted for his fine voice, his energy of style, and the decided manner in which he advocates his views. He has rendered good service on several important standing committees, especially upon that on Elections.

SPENCER MARLIN,

The Liberal Representative from Webster, was born in Sumner county, Tennessee, April 7th, 1814, though he has been a resident of Missouri for nearly half a century. In the fall of 1820 his family removed to this State settling in Marion county, where he remained with them for thirteen years, when he removed to what is now the county of Webster, of which he has ever since been a citizen. In 1866 he was elected a member of the county court of his adopted county, in which capacity he continued to serve up to the fall of 1870, when he was chosen to represent the county in the popular branch of the present Assembly. Politically, Judge Marlin is a Republican of the liberal school, and by calling, an unpretentious farmer. Though, I believe, he has never occupied the floor since a member of the House, he has been closely observant of all that has transpired during session hours, and prepared to vote on all questions with good judgment.

H. D. MARSHALL.

No member of the present House has been a more earnest laborer in the work of retrenchment and reform than the capable and conscientious Representative from Putnam. The onorous duties imposed on him by the Speaker in his appointment to the chairmanship of the committee especially charged with the consideration of questions of legislative economy, have been performed with untiring assiduity and fidelity, and many of the most important measures of the session looking to the relief of the taxpayer, owe their success to his individual efforts. Mr. Marshall is a Virginian, having been born in Franklin county, of that commonwealth, November 30th, 1830. In 1838 his family emigrated to Mississippi, and after a sojourn of four years in that State, removed to Missouri locating in what is now Putnam, but was at that time Adair county. Here the present Representative grew up to manhood, and has since continued to reside. His official career which has been a long as well as an honorable one, commenced in 1859, in which year he was appointed assessor of his adopt-

ed county. In the fall of the same year he also was elected clerk of the county court, which position he continued to hold for eleven consecutive years, and until elected to the seat he fills in the Twenty-sixth Assembly. In politics formerly an Old Line Whig, he has since the war been a conservative Republican, and is at present a zealous member of the Liberal faction of that party. His only participation in the late unpleasantness was in the capacity of quartermaster of the 45th Missouri regiment, a position to which he was appointed in 1864, and in which he served one year. As a member of the House, he has been a hard but quiet worker. Besides filling the chairmanship of the Committee on Retrenchment and Reform, he has also served as chairman of the Committee on Swamp Lands, and as a member of the special committees on the revenue and the judical redistricting of the State.

S. F. MARTIN,

Who sits as the Representative from Caldwell in the present House, is a native of Illinois, having been born in Marion county, in that State, January 25th, 1826. In 1838 his father removed with his family to Iowa, where the present Representative continued to reside up to 1850, when he crossed the plains and spent three years in the gold regions of California. Returning from the Pacific seaboard, he again took up his residence in the Hawkeye State, where he remained up to 1867, when he came to Missouri settling in the county whose interests have been intrusted to his charge in the popular branch of the Twenty-sixth Assembly. He has at various times followed the callings of farmer, merchant and mechanic, in all of which he has applied that energy for which he is characterized. He has filled numerous offices of a local character, and is at present President of the Board of Education of the town of Hamilton, in his adopted county. Since a member of the House he has taken a lively interest and an active and intelligent part in the proceedings of that body, and has exhibited an unfailing devotion to his duties. He has served as a member of the Committees on the Library and on Fees and Salaries. Politically, Mr. Martin is a Republican, though at all times tolerant of the views of those who differ with him.

JOHN I. MARTIN.

The self-made man, is the true hero, and to no one sitting in the present House is the term self-made more applicable than to the youthful member who represents the Ninth district of St. Louis. Mr. Martin owes his success to none but himself. Those obstacles which others have regarded as insuperable, he has quietly surmounted. In his lexicon there has not been nor is there such word as fail. Born in St. Louis May 24th, 1848, he is among the younger, with two exceptions, the youngest member of the House. His success proves his merit. Born of poor parents, and left almost from infancy to his own resource he has without the factitious aids by which others have risen made his way up from the driver of a dray in the streets of his native city to a seat in the legislative halls of the State, as the Representative of one of its wealthiest and most intelligent communities. To give the vicissitudes through which he has passed in reaching his present station, would exceed the space allotted in the present volume. The elements of success which he has possessed from the first, and which have especially marked his course at the Capital, are recognized and appreciated by his associates. His refined social impulses, his polished manners, his unspotted purity of life, and I may be pardoned for adding, his comely and prepossessing personal appearance, give him popularity wherever he is known. Since in the House he has served as a member of a number of important committees, and as the chairman of the Committee on Enrolled Bills, has discharged the duties attached to that position with marked fidelity and promptness. Though he seldom indulges in the debates, when he does so, the vivacity and vigor of his thoughts as well as his delivery always secure for him an attentive hearing. Politically, Mr. Martin is a zealous Democrat.

W. O. MAUPIN,

Representing the old, populous and Democratic county of Saline, is a native of Virginia, having been born in Albemarle county, in that State, October 17th, 1808. After graduating with honor from the university of his native State, he commenced the study of the law, and being admitted to the bar, followed for several years the practice of his profession in Albemarle and the adjoining counties. In 1837 he was united in marriage to the daughter of H. H. McDowell, Esq., a lady of great personal beauty and varied accomplishments, and two years thereafter emigrated to Missouri, locating in Saline county when that locality was comparatively an unreclaimed wilderness. Devoting the first three years of his residence in his new home to the practice of his profession, he abandoned it at the end of that time to engage in farming, a calling which he has since continued to follow. Commencing with the office of justice of the peace he has at various times filled almost every position in the gift of his immediate constituency. After serving for a number of years as a judge of the county court of his county, he was in 1850 elected to a seat in the lower branch of the Legislature, and in 1852 re-elected to the same position. In 1862 he was elected a member of the Senate from his district, embracing the populous and intelligent counties of Saline, Lafayette and Pettis. During his second term in the House he was chairman of the Committee on Agricultur, and as such was the author of the admirable report on the establishment of a State agricultural society at Boonville, from which has since sprung the numerous county societies of a similar character which ramify the whole State. The fact that in those days ten thousand copies of this paper were ordered by the House to be printed, is perhaps the highest, compliment that could have been paid its author. As a member of the present Assembly to which he was chosen in the fall of 1870, Mr. Maupin has fully availed himself of the experience gained in the earlier days of his official career, and has taken an active and intelligent part in the proceedings of the body in which he sits. He has done valuable service as chairman of the Committees on Roads and Highways and Federal Relations, and as a member of the Committees on Internal Improvements, Manufactures, and Benevolent and Seientific Institutions. He is, perhaps, the truest type at present sitting in either wing of the Capital, of the gentleman of the old school. A native of the Old Dominion, he is, despite his long residence in the West, still essentially Virginian in instinct as well as in manners.

P. MABREY,

The capable member from Ripley, is a native of Rockingham county North Carolina, where he was born in 1815. Shortly after his birth his family removed to Tennessee, where the remainder of his youth was spent and where he continued to reside up to 1838, when he emigrated to Missouri. Almost constantly since his advent in this State he has filled some position of honor and emolument. Settling first at Cape Girardeau he held respectively the office of justice of the peace and deputy, and afterwards county clerk of that county. Removing to the county of Wayne he was elected a justice of the peace here, also, besides acting as a district assessor and deputy circuit and county court clerk, and on the establishment of the probate and county court of that county, he was by appointment made its first judge. Settling in Stoddard county in 1860, he served again in the capacity of deputy clerk of the county court, and in 1866 was elected judge of the probate court, which position he continued to hold up to the following spring, when he was ousted upon a contest made before the circuit court of the county. Removing to Ripley county in 1868, he was, after a residence of only two years in that locality, elected to the seat he at present occupies in the House. In connection with his varied official duties, he has at various times followed the callings of merchant, miller and lumber dealer, in the latter of which he is at present engaged. Politically, Judge Mabrey is a Democrat of the strictest school, though in no instance has he permitted mere partisanship to interfere with his duties as a legislator. His seat in the House is seldom vacant, and its occupant is an attentive, though quiet observer of all that transpires during session hours. Of affable manners and the most generous impulses, he is universally popular among his associates.

THOMAS B. McALLISTER.

The Representative from Scotland county was born in the county of Campbell, of the "Old Dominion," in 1820. His father and family removed to Coshocton county, Ohio, in the year 1830, when that county was but sparsely settled. Here the present Representative received the greater part of his education, being compelled to walk four or five miles to the nearest school. In 1839, still clinging to the parental fold, he moved with his family to central Indiana, where he lead the life of a farmer until 1851, when he left his home and settled in Scotland county, Missouri, opening a farm upon the unbroken prairie near Memphis, the present county seat. Here he continued to reside up to the year 1861, when the war breaking out he entered the service, and continued therein up to the fall of that year, when he was badly wounded in a fight near Memphis, and being disabled for further active duty, was honorably discharged. In the fall of 1870 he made his entree into political life as the Liberal Republican candidate for the lower House of the present Assembly. As a legislator, he has been quiet and unostentatious, but not the less faithful and capable. While firm and consistent in his political opinions, he is very far from being a partisan, and both by his votes and his influence has evinced a manly independence and liberality. He has served as a member of the Committee on Accounts.

M. McMILLAN,

The Representative of the First district of Cooper county, was born in Livingston county, New York, and removed to Boonville, this State, in the year 1865. During a residence of five years in Boonville, as senior member of the law firm of McMillan Bros., he acquired such a widespread reputation as a leading lawyer that he was chosen to represent the 28th district in the State Senate, where he did effective service. He was afterward elected without opposition to represent the intelligent constituency of Cooper in the lower House of the Twenty-sixth General Assembly. A positive Republican and uncompromising in his advocacy of the distinctive principles of his party, his course in the House has been marked with honesty of purpose, courtesy towards opponents, and a liberality in discussion which have won for him the respect of his opponents. His arguments are ever marked by close, analytical arrangement and freedom from even the attempt at show. Possessing a clear, ringing voice and a fine command of language, whenever he addresses the Chair he commences, without prelude, to define his position by compact reasoning, rather than by appeals to prejudice or by flights of oratory. It is for this reason more, perhaps, than by his conceded record as an honest debater of unimpeachable moral rectitude, that he has assumed a position in the House not excelled by that of any of his party colleagues. On every important general measure, affecting the whole people of the State, and disconnected from party politics, Mr. McMillan has been found always at the front. He has been constantly in his seat, willing and ready to examine into all the details of legislation, freely interchanging his views with those who differed with him, and cheerfully submitting to the will of the majority.

JAMES McPIKE,

The venerable member from the Palmyra district of Marion county, differs quite as much from his younger colleague, Gen. Shields, in personal characteristics as he does in politics. One of the oldest, he has the further distinction also of being the wealthiest member of the House. But although in his sixty-seventh year, he is still active and energetic in the discharge of the duties imposed upon him, and is seldom absent either from his seat during session hours or from the committee room when his presence and services are required there. He is a native of Kentucky, from which State he immigrated to Missouri at an early date in her history. Though frequently elevated to official position by his immediate constituency, he has been a farmer all his life. Personally, he is a gentleman of unimpeachable integrity, sound practical sense, and much more than average ability. Though he never makes a set speech, and perhaps could not, were he to try, he is nevertheless a useful and valuable member. He is a true representative of the type of old school gentlemen who are fast passing away. His county could easily have sent a gentleman to the Capital who would have made more noise, but it is doubtful whether she could have sent one who would have been more highly respected by his associates, or have applied himself more faithfully to the discharge of his duties.

W. N. MILLER,

Representing the thoroughly Republican county of Douglas, is a native of East Tennessee, where he first saw the light April 10th, 1824. When twenty years of age he removed to Missouri, settling in what was then Ozark, but is now Douglas county, where he has since continued to reside. He has followed the callings of farming and milling, in the latter of which he is at present engaged. Taking strong grounds in favor of the Union on the outbreak of the late war, he entered the 16th regiment of Missouri volunteers, and served as a lieutenant in that command up to the restoration of peace. On the close of the war, or shortly thereafter, he was elected treasurer of his county, which office he continued to fill up to 1870, when elected to the seat he holds in the popular branch of the present Assembly. Politically, Mr. Miller is a Republican of the Radical school. He has, as a Representative, been always attentive to his duties, and his vote will be found recorded on almost every roll that has been called during the session.

JAMES M. MING,

The Representative from the Eastern district of Franklin, was born May 16th, 1824, in Campbell county, Virginia, and when thirteen years of age immigrated with his parents to Franklin county, Missouri. Here he assisted on the farm, and availed himself of the imperfect advantages to be had in a common country school, until he reached his sixteenth year, when he obtained a situation and entered a store at Port William as clerk, with his uncle, the late William North. On his uncle's removal to St. Louis, Mr. Ming became his successor, and continued the business for twenty years. During eighteen years of this time he was postmaster, and it is no slight proof of his close personal application to business, to say that every report and quarterly return to the department at Washington was made in his own handwriting. In 1864 he went on a trading expedition to Montana, and while there was a member of the board of aldermen of Virginia City. Returning to Missouri, he embarked as a wholesale dry goods merchant in St. Louis in the house of Barrows, House & Ming, from which he retired in 1868, since which time he has been engaged in farming and stock-raising. He was elected to the General Assembly in 1868, and again in 1870 ; the last time almost unanimously. His integrity, steady business habits and excellent social qualities make him a great favorite with his people ; though it is but justice to him to add that he has never sought office. Since in the House he has proven himself one of its most efficient members, attending strictly to all his duties, and although he does not appear as a speech-maker, he never misses a point of legislation. He is a most worthy representative of an intelligent people.

Z. J. MITCHELL,

Representing the Lexington district of Lafayette county, is among the younger members of the House, a native of Virginia, and in his bearing and general deportment does no discredit to the gallant Old Dominion. Under all circumstances—and a number of sharp encounters have tested him severely—he is the polished, courteous self-possessed gentleman. He is only twenty-eight years of age, but in that period has seen probably more of the world than even the oldest of his associates. After a partial completion of his collegiate course in his native State, which was interrupted by the breaking out of the late war, he repaired to Europe and renewed his studies at the University of Edinburg, from which ancient and famous institution he graduated with the degree of Master of Arts in 1865. While a student in Scotland he spent his vacations of some months annually in Germany and France, where he acquired to a considerable degree the languages of these countries, besides obtaining an insight into their social customs and political institutions. Having thus added immensely to his stock of practical and scholastic information, as well as having acquired much of that ease and polish of manner for which he is noted, he returned home, and shortly thereafter removed to Missouri and applied himself to the study of the law. On being admitted to the bar he at once applied himself to the practice of his profession, in which he is at present engaged at Lexington. Representing, as he does, one of the districts of Lafayette, it is hardly necessary to add that politically Mr. Mitchell is a Democrat. His course at the Capital has fully sustained the expectations of his friends. He has taken a prominent part in the proceedings of the body in which he sits, but while entertaining positive opinions on almost all subjects, and very frequently expressing them, he is still in no sense of the word dogmatic. As a speaker he is ready, fluent and continuous. In the distribution of the committees he was assigned by the Speaker to the chairmanship of Banks and Corporations, and made a member of the

Committees on the Judiciary, Insurance and the Lunatic Asylum. He is also a member of the special committee on redistricting the State into judicial circuits. He dresses in excellent good taste, is about five feet ten inches in hight, of light complexion, and possesses an intelligent and engaging countenance.

R. S. MOORE,

The Representative from Livingston county in the Twenty-fifth and also in the Twenty-sixth House, is a native of New York, having been born in Otsego county, that State, in 1831. When seven years of age he removed to the West with his parents, locating in Indiana. Here he followed the life of a farmer's boy, laboring in the summer and attending school in the winter, until he had reached his majority, when he became a student at Hanover, and afterwards at the university at Ann Arbor, Michigan, from which latter institution he graduated with honors in 1858. On completing his studies, he applied himself to school teaching in connection with the study of the law, and at the end of two years was admitted to the bar. Removing then to Missouri, and locating in Chillicothe, he commenced here the practice of his profession. Politically, Mr. Moore was a Democrat of the old Jefferson school, his father and grandfather having been of the same faith before him. Espousing Republicanism in 1862, he was in the following year elected by that party mayor of Chillicothe, and subsequently elected to the popular branch of the Twenty-fifth Assembly. He occupies his present seat as a Liberal of strong Democratic proclivities, having cast his vote for Gen. Blair for the Senate, rather than affiliate with the friends of Mr. Henderson in that contest. As a legislator, he is among the most experienced and best posted in the body, and, though at all times an active participant in the proceedings, is seldom, if ever, guilty of an infraction of the rules. He has been a capable and influential member of the important Committee on the Judiciary, and has served besides on a number of the more important special committees, and among others that appointed at the regular session to investigate the sale of the State bank stock to Capt. James B. Eads. Whatever duties have been imposed upon him have been promptly and conscientiously performed. In the more unrestrained social associations at the Capital, he has rendered himself a most agreeable companion, and is universally popular among his friends.

JAMES M. MOORE,

The Representative from Stone county, is a North Carolinian, having been born in that State May 13th, 1811. With his parents he removed to Tennessee in 1816, and came to Missouri in 1829, settling in Lawrence county, where he resided for thirty-six years. In 1861 he removed to Stone county, where he has continued to reside since. While a resident of Lawrence county he attained a wide popularity as an enterprising and honorable citizen, and for six years held the responsible office of sheriff also serving that constituency in the General Assembly. After his removal to Stone county, in 1861, he was elected county court justice, in which position he served with credit and distinction to himself and satisfaction to those who honored him. In 1862 he was elected captain of a company of Enrolled Militia of Missouri, and served in that capacity for fifteen months, when he was promoted to Major in the Fifty-second regiment. He was afterward detailed for duty with the Fifteenth Missouri cavalry. In all these positions he did excellent service, and bears many scars as relics of sharp encounters on the battle field. Since a member of the General Assembly he has ever been alive to the interests of his constituents, whom he serves with great fidelity, as well as ability. He was a Democrat up to the time of the war, but is now a Radical Republican, and announces his intention of so continuing.

N. A. MORTELL,

Representing the Tenth district of St. Louis, was born in the county of Cork, Ireland, in the year 1843, and is notable as the only native of the Emerald Isle occupying a seat in the present Democratic House. When only nine years of age he crossed the waters to seek his fortune in the New World, and on landing at New York, adopted and followed for three years the precarious life of a newsboy in that city. Having accumulated a few dollars in this calling, he set out in 1855 for the West, and located in Alton, Illinois, where he applied himself to learning the trade of a coppersmith. While engaged in this avocation, he attracted the attention of Col. Geo. B. Ingersoll, of Shipman, Illinois, by whom he was kindly taken from his uncongenial labor and sent to St. Paul's College, at Palmyra, Missouri, in which institution he acquired a thorough classical education. Having completed his studies, he took charge of the Cathedral school at Alton, and after a short term of service in this institution, removed to St. Louis and commenced the study of the law in the office of Judge Krum of that city. Since the completion of his legal studies and his admission to the bar, he has been actively engaged in the practice of his profession. Having received in 1870 the Democratic nomination for Representative of his district in the popular branch of the present Assembly, he was elected by a highly complimentary majority, and in the spring of 1871 received as further mark of the confidence and esteem of his party the nomination for city attorney of St. Louis, to which he was also elected by a handsome majority. Though aided in the acquirement of his education by his generous patron, Col. Ingersoll, Mr. Mortell is nevertheless, in a large measure, a self-made man, and the success he has achieved, both politically and professionally, is mainly due to his own exertions and honesty of purpose. As a speaker, he is fluent and logical, and since a member of the House, he has engaged freely in the discussions in that body. He has also done valuable service as a member of the important Committees on Banks and Corporations, the Judiciary, and the special committees of the St. Louis Delegation.

H. G. MULLINGS,

One of the best informed, as he is one of the oldest and most experienced members of the House, is the gentleman whose name appears above, and who, with Mr. Langston, represents the populous and intelligent county of Greene. A member of the Twenty-fourth, Twenty-fifth, and now of the Twenty-sixth Assembly, Mr. Mullings is thoroughly up in the business of the House, and may be said to have Jefferson's Manual fairly at his finger's ends. It would be difficult for the shrewdest to spring a parliamentary trap that would ensnare him, or get the House into a parliamentary snarl too intricate for his powers of extraction. A point of order is his ambition and "strongest hold." In view of this special qualification, he was by far the fittest person that the Republican side of the chamber could have put forward for the Speakership at the inception of the session, and if elected he would doubtless have filled the position with credit and satisfaction. As it is, he has done excellent service on the floor, and as the chairman of the Committee on Education, in which latter capacity his time has been largely applied with his associates to a revision of the present defective school law. Mr. Mullings is a native Missourian, and from boyhood has been a resident of the Southwest portion of the State, the peculiar interests of which he fully comprehends. In the late unpleasantness in the Republican household he went off with the bolters, though he has since resumed his relations to the party. Mr. Mullings is a ready, and generally fluent debater, and is frequently on the floor. Of a figure above the average hight, he commands attention when he first rises, and generally manages to retain it by what he says. He may be readily recognized by a heavy growth of sandy beard, a slight stoop of the shoulders and an air of ease, and, in a measure, of assurance which never forsakes him.

P. W. MURPHY.

Judge Murphy, as he is addressed by his friends, who represents in the House the great mineral county of St. Francois, is a native of the Old Dominion, having been born in Culpepper county on the 24th of December, 1820. After receiving a thorough education in the schools of his native State, he set out to seek his fortune in the West, and in 1844 located in Missouri, where he has since constantly resided. The first ten years of his residence in his new home was devoted to school teaching. At the close of this period taking a contract for grading a portion of the Iron Mountain railroad, he became identified with that important enterprise, to which he devoted his attention for several years. Subsequently to this he divided his time between farming and mining up to 1866, when he was elected to the office of assessor of taxes for St. Francois county. This position he held up to 1870, in the fall of which year he was chosen to represent his county in the popular branch of the present Assembly. Since his arrival at the Capital few gentlemen have more fully succeeded in securing and retaining the regard and confidence of their associates, or proven themselves more watchful guardians of the interests of their constituency. Though I believe he has never inflicted upon the House a set speech, he is frequently upon the floor, and is always listened to with attention and respect. Politically, Judge Murphy is a Democrat of the most uncompromising stripe. He is a member of the important Committee on Agriculture, in which capacity he has done excellent service, and also a member of the Committees on Retrenchment and Reform and on Fees and Salaries.

SAMUEL F. MURRAY,

Representing the Western district of the populous county of Pike, is a native of Loudoun county, Virginia, and fifty-six years of age. In 1840 he left home to seek his fortune in the West, and located at Troy, in Lincoln county, of this State. During the last two years of his residence in the Old Dominion, and the first three years in his new home, he was engaged in school teaching, and among his pupils were a number of gentlemen who have since attained the greatest prominence in their respective States. At the close of his career as a teacher he immediately commenced the study of the law, and in the year 1845 first commenced its practice in the county of Lincoln. In the same year he also purchased the Democratic paper of Pike county, and in the year 1846 removed with it to the city of Louisiana, in that county. In the year 1847 he was elected clerk of the county court of Pike county, and continued to edit and publish his paper for some five years thereafter, as well as to discharge the duties of his office as clerk. As an editor, he was always bold and fearless, and was a pioneer in the advocacy of the election of our Congressmen by districts, and of the State officers and Judges by the people. Before the expiration of the second term of his clerkship he was elected judge of probate to fill the vacancy in that office occasioned by the death of Judge Finley. He was re-elected in the year 1859, and filled the office till the close of the year 1862. He acted also for a time as county commissioner and county superintendent of common schools. In 1845 he was solicited by his democratic friends of Lincoln and St. Charles counties in caucus to submit his name for a nomination as a candidate for the Convention to make a new Constitution for the State, but declined. Though always ardent in support of political principles, he never could be induced to run for political office till the year 1870, when on the morning of the Democratic Convention he first consented to the use of his name for a nomination for the office of Representative in the present House for the purpose of advocating a local measure in which he felt great interest. During the time he held these county offices he also practiced law as far as he could without interfering with the discharge of his duties. Before the organization of the House he was prominently spoken of as Speaker of that body, but owing to feeble health declined to submit his name to the Democratic caucus. No member has been more assiduous in the discharge of his duties, and besides his services on the floor, he has acted as chairman of the important Committee on Criminal Jurisprudence.

A. W. MYERS.

No county of the State is better represented in the present House than the intelligent and populous county of Linn, in the person of the clear-headed, hard-working and practical member whose name occurs at the head of this sketch. Mr. Myers is a native of Ohio, having been born in Jefferson county, in that State, July 2d, 1824. In 1851 having completed his education and prepared himself for the practice of the law, he removed to the neighboring State of Indiana, and locating in Whitley county commenced the practice of that profession, which he continued to follow up to 1864, when he decided to change his residence, and with that view, left home on a prospecting tour. In the following year after having visited several of the Western States, he located at his present home in Missouri, where he resumed the practice of the law, and continued to apply himself to that profession up to 1870, since which time he has been successfully engaged in mining and manufacturing. In the same year he accepted the nomination which resulted in his election to a seat in the popular branch of the present Assembly. On the organization of the House, his superior abilities were recognized by Speaker Wilson, and he was assigned a place on the important Committees on Internal Improvements, Insurance, Mines and Mining, of which he has been an active and serviceable member, and over whose deliberations he has exercised a positive influence. He has also served as a member of the special committees on probate and common pleas courts, and the investigation of the military claims of the State. Though seldom on the floor he is by no means without opinions or the ability to express them and on questions of a practical character, he is freely and frequently consulted by his younger associates. Politically, Mr. Myers is a zealous and consistent Democrat.

THOMAS D. NEAL,

The member from Harrison, is a native of Kentucky, having been born in Franklin county, of that State, in 1840. In 1856, being then a lad of only sixteen years, he immigrated to Missouri, settling first in Daviess and subsequently in Gentry county. The only education he ever received was such as he could obtain in the private schools of his native State, as no free school system existed in Kentucky at that day. In politics, Mr. Neal has been a zealous Republican ever since the first organization of that party, and although surrounded in his new home by those who differed most widely with him in political sentiment, was even before the war a fearless and outspoken advocate of free-soilism. During the years 1859 and 1860 he was a frequent contributor to the columns of the Missouri *Democrat* and St. Joseph *Free Democrat*, and for his articles in the last named journal especially aroused a sentiment of hostility against him, which ultimately compelled him to leave his adopted county. On forsaking Gentry, he removed to Harrison county, where he engaged in school teaching and continued to follow that calling up to the outbreak of the late war, when at the first call for troops he entered the service and continued therein up to the close of hostilities. He was in numerous actions with his command in Missouri, Arkansas and Georgia, and in one engagement in Boone county, in this State, was severely wounded. On being mustered out of the service in September, 1865, he renewed his residence in Harrison county and established the North Missouri *Tribune*, a Radical Republican newspaper, at Bethany, in that county, which he has since continued to publish. In connection with his journalistic duties he also commenced the study of the law, and in 1868 was admitted to the practice of that profession. He has filled various civil offices, commencing with a seat in the board of aldermen in Bethany in 1866. In 1869 he was elected probate judge of Harrison county, in 1868, elected a member of the House in the Twenty-fifth Assembly, and in 1870 re-elected to the seat which he at present occupies. Since at the Capital he has, besides his labors during session hours, served as a member of the Committees on Banks and Corporations and the Penitentiary. Possessing a large fund of information, and being a ready and easy speaker, he has participated freely in the debates of the session, while with an occasional flash of wit he has repeatedly provoked the House as well as the lobby to laughter. In this manner he has not unfrequently carried a point when the soundest reasoning would have failed.

A. G. NEWMAN.

Judge Newman, who, with his junior in years, Mr. Bass, represents the old and populous county of Boone, was born in Augusta county, Virginia, November 4th, 1808. After spending his youth and earlier manhood in his native State, he removed in 1834 to Tennessee locating in the town of Greenville, where he continued to reside up to 1837. During his residence here he became the intimate personal and political friend of ex-President Johnson, at that period in the eventful life of the latter, when he was about placing his foot on the first round of the official ladder to the top of which he eventually ascended. In 1837, leaving Tennessee he made a brief sojourn in the neighboring State of Alabama, and subsequently removed to Missouri settling in Clay county, and after a residence of two years in that locality removing to Boone county, where he has since continued to make his home. Though his present occupation is that of a practical tinner, he has at different times followed various avocations, and made and lost several fortunes. Though always taking a lively interest in public affairs, and an active politician, since attaining his majority, the only office he has ever held at the hands of his party or his people is that which he at present holds as a member of the Twenty-sixth Assembly. His legislative record has been characterized by a faithful discharge of the duties imposed on him, either during session hours or in the committee room, and an especial regard for the interests and requirements of his own county. Politically, he is a life-long Democrat.

W. H. NORRIS.

One of the oldest and most experienced members of the present House is the worthy member from Ozark county. The acceptable manner in which he has served his constituency has kept him at the Capital as the guardian of their interests for a long term of years. Mr. Norris is thirty-six years of age, and a native of Kentucky, though a resident of Missouri since boyhood. By calling, he is a farmer, and politically, a Republican. In addition to his constant participation in the business of the House, he has served faithfully as a member of the Committee on the Blind Asylum.

G. W. O'BANNAN,

Representing the county of Dallas, was born in that county, January 15th, 1842, and raised on a farm. Entering the service immediately on the outbreak of the late war he continued therein up to the restoration of peace, serving with the rank of lieutenant. In 1866 he was appointed postmaster of the town of Buffalo, in his native county, and held that office about one year, and in 1870 was elected to a seat in the lower House of the Twenty-sixth Assembly. Politically, Mr. O'Bannan is a Republican, and by calling a merchant. He has been a quiet but nevertheless attentive and serviceable member of the body in which he sits, and votes with good judgment and a conscientious regard for the interests of his constituency. He has been a serviceable member of the Committee on Militia.

A. O'BANNON,

The worthy member from Pettis, is fifty-five years of age, and is also a native and life-long resident of Missouri, with whose interests and the demands of whose people he is thoroughly acquainted. Few gentlemen enjoy to a greater degree personal popularity among their constituency, and few, by the probity and rectitude of their lives, are more deserving of the good opinions of their associates. A farmer by calling, and without political or official aspirations, he has nevertheless been frequently honored with preferment to places of public trust. After serving acceptably as a justice of the county court of Pettis, he received in 1870 the nomination which resulted in his election to a seat in the present House by a highly complimentary majority. Politically, Mr. O'Bannon is a Republican of the liberal school, and as such was generally supported by the Democracy of his county. Since at the Capital he has seldom been out of his seat on any account, except sickness, and has faithfully and conscientiously applied himself to the discharge of all the duties devolving upon him. He has served as a member of several important committees.

P. J. PAULEY,

The popular and capable member from the First representative district of St. Louis, is a native of Prussia, and first saw the light May 23d, 1832. In his fourteenth year his parents immigrated to the United States, and located in St. Louis, where the present Representative has ever since made his home. Adopting in early life the calling of a machinist, he has continued to follow that avocation, and is at present at the head of one of the largest iron establishments of St. Louis. While giving the closest attention to his private affairs, however, he has always taken a deep interest and active part in local and State politics, and has for a number of years been an efficient and influential member of both the State and County Central Democratic committees. Of the former he has been a member since 1863, and with his associates co-operated in bringing about the important political revolution, which resulted in the reinstatement of the disfranchised classes in 1870. But while devoting his efforts, and much of his time, to the advancement of his party, he has neither sought or held any office within its gift, prior to his seat in the popular branch of the present Assembly. His course, since at the Capital, has been marked by a conscientious regard for the public welfare, and especially, the interests of his immediate constituency. Though seldom occupying the floor, he generally entertains positive opinions, and votes on all questions with good judgment. He has served as chairman of the Committee on Manufactures and as a member of the special committee of the St. Louis Delegation.

W. S. POPE.

Maj. Pope, who represents the Fourth district of St. Louis in the present House, is a native of Kentucky, having been born in Christian county, in that State, in 1829. When a lad he removed with his parents to Illinois, where he was placed at work on a farm, a calling he continued to follow until by his own unaided efforts he had acquired education sufficient to enable him to teach school. After teaching for two years, and in the meantime continuing his own studies he entered upon a collegiate course, and finally perfected his education in the classical and scientific branches, besides mastering several of the modern languages. Shortly after graduating he was elected a professor in Rock River Seminary, one of the oldest schools in Northern Illinois, and for six years was a teacher of mathematics and the German language in that institution. While in the discharge of these duties he also gave a portion of his time to the study of the law, and on abandoning his chair as a professor was admitted to the practice. On the outbreak of the late war, which occurred shortly after his being admitted to the bar, he was called to the State Capital and appointed by Gov. Yates as an aid on the staff of that official. After a short service in this capacity he was appointed a paymaster in the army, and in the latter office served to the close of the war. On the restoration of peace he removed to St. Louis, where he has since been successfully engaged in the practice of his profession. Accepting in 1870 the nomination of the Liberal Republicans of his district for Representative, he was elected by a complimentary majority to the seat he holds in the popular branch of the present Assembly. A ready and continuous speaker, and possessing a fund of information on almost every subject of legislation, he has engaged frequently in the debates of the session and aided greatly in perfecting various measures during their consideration by the House. In addition to his labors during session hours he has also done valuable service as chairman of the Committee on Benevolent and Scientific Institutions, and as a member of the Committee on Education.

WILLIAM PRICE.

No county has had greater difficulty in securing representation in the present House, or is finally better represented, than the good county of Newton. Mr. Price, who by a second special election occupies the seat rendered vacant early in the regular session by the death of Gen. Beeman, is a native of Tennessee, having first seen the light in Williamson county, of that State, February 22d, 1831. At an early age, however, his family removed to Weakley county, in the same State, where his youth was spent, and where he continued to reside up to 1853, when he immigrated to Missouri, and settled in Newton county, his present home. Since in Missouri he has followed the calling of a merchant, leading a quiet and unpretentious life, though at all times taking a lively interest in public affairs, and entertaining strong political convictions. In 1854 he was appointed to the responsible position of treasurer of his adopted county, which he continued to hold, however, for a short time only, and this with the seat he at present occupies in the House are the only public offices which he has ever filled, or to which, I believe, he has ever aspired. As a Representative he has been attentive to the business of the body, faithful in the discharge of all duties immediately devolving upon him, and has made a record which cannot fail to receive the indorsement of his constituency irrespective of party. Coming into the House after the organization, the only committee to which he has been assigned has been that of Fees and Salaries, of which he has proven a valuable member. Politically, Mr Price is a Democrat.

J. P. RANEY,

In whom the county of Wright has found a capable and conscientious Representative in the popular branch of the present Assembly, is a native of Kentucky, and thirty-nine years of age. After spending his youth in his native State, he immigrated to Missouri and located in Dade county. At the outbreak of the late war he entered the service and continued therein up to the cessation of hostilities, serving gallantly with the rank of lieutenant. On the restoration of peace he returned to Missouri and located in Barry county, where, in 1866, he was elected to the office of sheriff of the county, which position he held for two years. In 1868 he removed to Wright county, where he has since resided, and with whose interests he has become thoroughly acquainted and identified. A Democrat up to the outbreak of the late war, he acted with the Republican party until 1870, when he gave in his adhesion to the Liberal cause, and as the nominee of that party was elected to his present seat in the House. Since at the Capital his course has been marked by close attention to the business of the body, liberality of political sentiment and geniality of manners that have rendered him universally popular among his associates.

WILLIAM RANDALL,

Representing the Second district of Buchanan county, was born in the State of New York, in the year 1833. He came to Missouri at an early age, and has ever since been engaged in the occupation of farming. During the late war he was a captain of Militia in the State service, and in the fall of 1870 was nominated for member of the House of Representatives by the Liberal Republicans of his district. The Democrats made no opposition, and he was elected by a handsome majority over his opponent—an extreme Radical. Captain Randall being one of the wealthiest farmers of his section of country, has long been recognized as a gentleman of influence, and is universally regarded as a man of the strictest integrity. He is a member of the Committee on Roads and Highways, and has taken great interest in all matters relating to the welfare of the agricultural community.

WILLIAM RAY.

Captain Ray, on whom it has twice devolved to represent the county of Barry in the popular branch of the Legislature, was born in Granger county, Tennessee, November 14th, 1834, and a resident of that State up to 1858, when he removed to Missouri and located in Barry county, where he has since continued to make his home. Taking a positive position in favor of the Union at the inception of the late war between the States, he entered the service and continued therein as a captain in the 15th Missouri regiment up to the close of hostilities. In 1863, while still holding his military commission, he was elected sheriff of his adopted county, and discharged the responsible duties of that office for two years, and at the expiration of his sheriffalty was elected a member of the lower branch of the Twenty-third Assembly. While holding his seat in that body he also continued to hold his commission in the army, and when not engaged at the Capital, was in active service with his regiment in the field. On being mustered out of the service in July, 1865, he returned to his civil pursuits—farming and stock raising—in his adopted county, to which he continued to give his undivided attention up to 1870, when he again entered the political arena and was elected to his present seat in the House. An experienced legislator, and thoroughly familiar with the rules, he has taken an intelligent, though quiet and unobtrusive part in the proceedings of the body. He has also served efficiently as a member of the Committee on Militia. Politically, Capt. Ray is a life-long Democrat, and will lose no fair opportunity to strengthen his party in the State, though never permitting mere partisanship to interfere with his duties as a legislator.

ALLEN P. RICHARDSON,

Representing the Second district of the populous county of Franklin, was born in Lawrenceburg, Anderson county, Kentucky, November 10th, 1822, and immigrated to Missouri with his parents in 1830, settling in Ray county, where he continued to reside until twenty-four years of age. His parents were both natives of Kentucky, and his father, Capt. John C. Richardson, a soldier of the war of 1812, and distinguished himself in many of the engagements that decided the issue of that struggle in favor of American arms. The education of Mr. Richardson was completed at Boone Femme College, in Boone county, of this State, in 1844. In 1846 he was married in Ray county to Miss Fannie, eldest daughter of ex-Governor Austin A. King, and in 1849 was appointed Register of State Lands under the administration of that gentleman. He thus came into public life at the early age of twenty-four, and amid the exciting discussions growing out of the passage of the celebrated Jackson resolutions from which the great Senator Col. Benton took his appeal, but notwithstanding his youth, he assumed a prompt, decided and prominent position against the resolutions under the leadership of Senator Benton, and by this course won many warm political friends in the spirited contest of that period. In 1852 he was nominated on the Democratic State ticket, of which Gen. Sterling Price was the head, and elected to fill for a second term the office of Register of Lands. In 1856 he was renominated also for the same office on what was known, at that time, as the Benton ticket, but after a vigorous canvass was in this instance defeated, there being three tickets in the field. Taking a positive stand in favor of the unity of the States on the outbreak of the late war, he organized and assumed command of a regiment of ninety days' men, and at the expiration of his term of service, he was appointed by Gov. Gamble, State Paymaster, with the rank of captain. Having filled this office for about one year, he was in 1862 elected to the State Senate from the Jefferson City district, and as a member of that body distinguished himself by his opposition to the calling of a Constitutional Convention, looking to the immediate emancipation of slavery in the State and the overthrow of the provisional government. In 1865 he made a vigorous canvass of the central portion of the State against the adoption of the Constitution which was in that year submitted to the people, and in the following year ran again for the Senate, but was defeated. In 1868 he was chosen an elector on the Seymour and Blair ticket, and in the following year removed to Franklin county, by whose people he was in 1870 honored with the seat he occupies in the present House. Since at the Capital his usefulness, has in a measure, been impaired by feeble health, notwithstanding which, he has, however, taken an active and prominent part in the deliberations of the body, besides doing valuable service as chairman of the Committee on Claims, and as a member of the Committee on Internal Improvements. He is frequently on the floor, and is always listened to with that respect and attention to which his experience as a legislator entitles him.

H. K. S. ROBINSON.

Though among the quiet and modest members of the House, no gentleman on the Republican side of the chamber has given closer attention to the business of the body or been in his seat to respond more frequently to the call of the roll, than the worthy member from the county of Holt. Mr. Robinson is a native of Ohio, and was born in Ross county, of that State, October 11th, 1835. The first eighteen years of his life were spent on a farm, after which he both attended and taught school. Subsequently he also followed the avocations of a clerk and a book-keeper in a banking house. On the outbreak of the late war, he recruited a company and entered the service as a lieutenant. In the memorable engagement before

Atlanta, in 1864, he was severely wounded, and still carries a minnie ball in his right shoulder. As a recognition of his gallantry in this action, he was commissioned a captain, but shortly thereafter compelled to abandon the service on account of his wounds. Returning to his native State in the spring of 1865, he removed in the fall of the same year to Missouri and settled in Holt county, where he has since continued to reside, and where he is at present engaged in mercantile pursuits. His first entrance into the political arena was in 1870, in the fall of which year he was elected on the Republican ticket in his county to the seat he fills in the present Assembly. Making no pretentions whatever to oratory, he has refrained from taking part in the debates of the session, though generally well informed on all questions under consideration, and prepared to vote according to his convictions. He has served efficiently as a member of the Committee on Benevolent and Scientific Institutions.

W. F. ROLSTON,

Representing the county of Johnson, is a native of Kentucky, having been born in Hart county, of that commonwealth, October 16th, 1825. On the outbreak of the Mexican war he entered the service, and continued therein to the restoration of peace as a Kentucky volunteer. In 1849, leaving his native State he removed to Missouri, locating first in Ray county, and after a sojourn of seventeen years in that locality, changed his residence to Johnson county, where he has since continued to make his home. Taking strong grounds in favor of the preservation of the Union he entered the army at the inception of the late war between the States, and served gallantly to the close as a lieutenant in the 51st Missouri regiment. The only civil office he has ever held is his present seat in the House. Since at the Capital he has been rarely out of his seat, and his name will be found recorded on nearly every roll that has been called during the session. He has also been a laborious member of the Committee on Local Bills. Politically, Mr. Rolston is a Republican of the Liberal school, and by calling a farmer.

CHARLES W. SAMUEL

Representing the "Kingdom of Callaway," is a native Missourian, having been born in Palmyra, Marion county, December 15th, 1830. His parents were both Kentuckians, and his father, who was a physician, died in 1833 of cholera, contracted while in the discharge of his professional duties. After this early bereavement the present Representative was taken by his mother to Callaway county, where the remainder of his youth was spent. In his new home his time was divided between attending school and working on a farm up to 1847, when he went into a dry goods house as a clerk. After following this business for three or four years, he crossed the plains to California, and spent one year in the gold regions, at the expiration of that time, returning home by way of Central America and Havana. On his arrival in his native State, he located at Columbia, Boone county, where he sojourned up to 1853, when he returned to Callaway county and embarked in business for himself as a dry goods merchant, a calling in which he has been actively engaged ever since. In 1864 he was appointed postmaster of Cedar City, but resigned in the following year. In 1866 he was reappointed and held the position up to 1870, when he again resigned. In 1868 he was a candidate for a seat in the popular branch of the Twenty-fifth Assembly, but the registrars being of a very different political faith from himself, refused to register him, and he withdrew from the contest. On receiving a renomination in 1870, he was elected to the seat he occupies in the Twenty-sixth Assembly by a handsome majority. Though an Old-Line Whig during the existence of that party, he has, under the new order of things, been a consistent adherent to the principles of Democracy. Few gentlemen have made a better record at the Capital, or have acted on all subjects with a more scrupulous regard for the best interests of their constituency and the State at large. Though seldom taking the floor, when he does so, he never fails to secure an attentive hearing of his views, and generally carries his points. In addition to his services during the session hours, he has also been an assiduous laborer in the committee room, having served as chairman of the Committee on the Deaf and Dumb and Lunatic Asylums, and the committee to investigate the affairs of the 81st and 82d regiments of militia, besides being a member of the Committee on Retrenchment and Reform.

LINUS SANFORD.

A brighter or pleasanter face cannot be found on the Democratic side of the chamber than that of the intelligent and accomplished gentleman who sits in the present Assembly as the Representative of the old county of Cape Girardeau. Mr. Sanford is a native of Missouri and of the county whose interests have been intrusted to him at the Capital, having been born in that locality January 1st, 1838. Having received a thorough preparatory education, he completed his scholastic studies at St. Vincent's College, and on leaving that institution entered the law department of the famous University of Harvard, at Cambridge, Massachusetts. On graduating from the latter school, he was, in 1861, admitted to the bar, and has since that date been successfully engaged in the practice of his profession in his native county, where he has achieved a reputation scarcely second to any at that bar. Though a zealous and active Democrat, and possessing the highest qualifications, the only political position to which he has aspired or has ever held, is his present seat in the House. To those who know him most intimately, the probable secret of this fact is readily discoverable in his unassuming ability and modest worth, which, while they constitute the best qualification, are but seldom apt to secure political preferment. Since a member of the House these traits of his character have especially marked his legislative course, and though rarely absent from his seat, and thoroughly informed on all that transpires in the hall, he has seldom occupied the floor, and never, I believe, made a set speech. In the committee room he has been an earnest but quiet worker, and as a member of the important Committee on the Judiciary has done especially good service.

C. A. SCHOOLEY,

The member from St. Clair, was born in Union county, Pennsylvania, January 22d, 1841, where his youth and early manhood were spent, and where he received a good academic education. In 1860 he emigrated from his native State to Nebraska, where he resided for one year and until the late war broke out, when he entered the Federal army as a private soldier. In 1863 he was for gallant conduct commissioned a lieutenant and assigned to duty on the staff of Gen. Chetland, and in 1864 promoted to a captaincy, with which rank he served to the close of hostilities, being finally mustered out in July, 1865. On the restoration of peace, he removed to Missouri and located in Sedalia, where he commenced the practice of the law. Remaining here until 1869, he in that year removed to St. Clair county, where he has since made his home and where he is at present engaged in farming and milling. In the recent dissensions in the Republican party, he espoused the cause of Liberalism, and received the nomination which resulted in his election to the seat he at present holds in the House. His course at the Capital has been such as to secure for him the esteem of his associates and the indorsement of his constituency. Though a quiet he has been an intelligent and hard-working member. He has been a member of the Committee on Swamp Lands.

FREDERICK SCOVILLE.

The acknowledged leader of the Republican majority in the last House, whom a lucrative Federal appointment afterwards removed to New Mexico, is succeeded in the Twenty-sixth Assembly by Fred. Scoville, of Ray county. This gentleman, upon whom Judge Waters' legislative mantle has fallen, and who occupies the same desk, is also his partner in the practice of law, a gentleman of fine legal attainments, and in every respect, except politically, is quite as efficient a Representative of his constituents, and enjoys quite as fully the respects and esteem of his associates as his more noted predecessor. A native of New York, where he was born in 1834, Mr. Scoville came to Missouri in 1865, and located in the flourishing town of Richmond, in Ray county, where he has since resided, and with whose interests he has become thoroughly acquainted and identified. A gentleman of retiring disposition, modestly deferential to those of larger experience, it is perhaps only in the committee room and among his personal associates that his real worth and ability are known and properly appreciated. He has, I believe, but once during the session occupied the floor of the House, his only speech being made in opposition to the calling of a Convention to revise the present Constitution. The fact that this effort has not been followed by a second cannot, however, be attributed to his inability to favorably impress his hearers, but rather to his native modesty and a reluctance to thrust himself into notice at the expense of that respect from his associates, which his quiet and dignified reserve have won for him. In committee labor few men are more industrious, and it is here that his efforts and abilities have been applied with signal fidelity. Like his predecessor, Mr. Scoville is a Republican.

J. W. SHAFER,

The member from Shelby, is a native of Livingston county, New York, thirty-seven years of age, and a lawyer by profession, having been admitted to the bar at Rochester, in his native State, in 1857. Immigrating to the West in 1859, he located in Indiana and continued to reside in that State up to the outbreak of the late war. At the first call for troops he entered the service as a private soldier of the 19th Indiana regiment, and continued therein up to the cessation of hostilities, participating in nearly all the important engagements of the army of the Potomac, and finally being mustered out in July, 1865, with the rank of Lieut. Colonel. On the restoration of peace he removed to Missouri, and settled in Shelby county, where he has since been successfully engaged in the practice of his profession. Politically, a Democrat before the war, a Republican during the war and up to 1870, he has since that date been a zealous member of the Liberal party with strong proclivities towards his early political faith. Elected in the fall of 1870 to a seat in the present House, he has taken an active part in the proceedings of that body, and it is safe to say that no measure of importance, and especially any affecting the interest of the tax-payer, has escaped his careful scrutiny, and when not in accordance with his convictions encountered vigorous opposition. A ready and easy speaker, he has probably occupied the floor more frequently than any member of the body, and though not always successful in carrying his points, has placed himself on record on almost every question which has entered into the debates of the session. He has also done valuable service as a member of the Committee on County Boundaries, and is especially known at the Capital as an earnest advocate of the political as well as the social rights of woman.

JOHN SHARP,

The worthy Representative from the county of Schuyler, is a native of Ohio, forty-six years of age, a farmer by calling, and in politics a Liberal Republican. Though reserved and reticent, seldom occupying the floor of the House or the columns of the official paper, he is nevertheless a sharp observer of all that transpires in the hall, and a faithful guardian of the interests of his immediate constituency and the State, while his many amiable and kindly qualities of heart have rendered him universally popular among his associates. He has served efficiently as a member of the Committee on Mines and Mining.

M. C. SHEWALTER,

One of the younger members of the House, ably representing the Eastern district of Lafayette county in the present Assembly, was born in Jefferson county, West Virginia, and is about thirty years of age. With good common school opportunities in his youth, he made commendable progress, and at the age of twelve years removed with his parents to Missouri, locating in Saline county. Here he availed himself of the ordinary means of obtaining an education, occasionally teaching school. In 1859 he entered McKee College, in Macon county, remaining there until the outbreak of the late war. Immediately at the close of the war he completed a course of law study, was admitted to practice, and soon after removed to Lafayette county, locating in Waverly. In 1868 he received the Democratic nomination of his district for a seat in the popular branch of the General Assembly, and was defeated by a small majority. In 1869 he formed a law partnership and commenced practice. In 1870 he was renominated as a Democrat for a seat in the House of Representatives, upon a fusion ticket, and was elected by a handsome majority to the position which he has since filled with marked ability. As a debater—and a number of sharp parliamentary encounters have developed his powers—he has probably no superior in the House. With a clear, ringing voice, an ornate and finished diction, he combines a logical and discriminating mind and a rich, almost luxuriant fancy. He, undoubtedly, gives rare promise as one of the rising young men of the State. He is chairman of the important Committee on Printing, and a member of the Committee on Constitutional Amendments, besides having served on various special committees.

GEO. H. SHIELDS,

The member from the Hannibal district of Marion county, is a native of Kentucky, having been born in Bardstown, in that State, June 19th, 1842. When he was only two years old his parents immigrated to Missouri and settled in Hannibal, where he has ever since resided, and with whose interests he has become thoroughly acquainted and identified. After a thorough academic education he perfected himself in the classics at Westminster College, at Fulton, in this State, and subsequently graduated in law at the Louisville University. Entering the military service at the outbreak of the late war, he served to the close, rising from the rank of lieutenant to that of major. Since the restoration of peace, he has applied himself to the practice of the law, and probably there are few members of the bar in the State who, at his age, have made a more extended reputation. As a recognition of his qualifications in this direction he was elected city attorney of Hannibal in 1866, and re-elected to the same position in 1867 and 1868 without opposition, declining a third renomination in 1869. He was in 1868 put forward by his friends for a seat in the popular branch of the Twenty-fifth Assembly, but owing to the death of one of his family withdrew from the race. Being nominated again in 1870, he was elected by a highly complimentary majority, and is the only McClurg Republican at present sitting in the House from the Hannibal district. But though a Radical, and while his Democratic associates find little congenial to their taste in his political creed, his professional talent and amiable qualities as a gentleman are generally recognized, and have rendered him popular with all parties at the Capital. Possessing a finished education, with fine command of language, forcible in argument, and accustomed to public speaking, he has taken a prominent part in the legislation of the session, and as an able and effective speaker and logical reasoner always commands the attention of the House when he takes the floor. His untiring energy and intellectual ability have entitled him to be regarded as one of the leaders of his party at the Capital; and as chairman of the important Committee on Constitutional Amendments, and a member of the Judiciary and various special committees, he has equally distinguished himself in the discharge of his duties in the committee room and on the floor of the House. As a mark of the respect and esteem entertained for him by the Republicans, he, though a very young man, was unanimously elected permanent chairman of the Republican State Convention held in Jefferson City, February 22d, 1872, over several distinguished competitors. His youth was one of the arguments used against his election, on the ground that only a person of years and large experience could control the large assemblage. The result of Mr. Shields' election, however, did any thing but verify this prediction. The skillful and impartial manner in which he performed the difficult task aided greatly in promoting the perfect order and harmony which prevailed, and won encomiums from those who, in the beginning, were his strongest opponents.

MARION SIDES,

The estimable gentleman and worthy member from Dent, is a native Missourian, having first seen the light in Perry county, January 27th, 1837, in which locality his youth was spent, and where he continued to reside up to 1861. Among the first to respond to the call for troops for the late civil war, he entered the service as a private soldier, and served gallantly to the close, being mustered out with the rank of lieutenant. On the restoration of peace he changed his residence from Perry to Dent county, where he has since continued to make his home, and with whose interests he has become thoroughly identified. As an appreciation of his merits he was chosen by his associates in his new home to represent them in the Twenty-fifth Assembly, and the acceptability of his services in that body secured for him in 1870 a renomination and re-election to a seat in the present House. As a member of the Twenty-sixth Assembly he has fully availed himself of his previous legislative experience and proven an active and most useful, as he is also a most conscientious member. He has been the author of a number of important measures, and among them the bill to prevent discrimination and extortion by railroad companies in the matter of freight charges. He has also served as a member of the Committees on the Library and Enrolled Bills. Politically, a zealous Democrat, he has nevertheless warm friends in all parties.

R. T. SLOAN,

The clear-headed and capable member from the county of Worth, is a native of Suckerdom, having been born in Vermillion county, of that State, July 23d, 1833. After receiving a thorough academic education, he commenced the study of the law and fitted himself for the practice of that profession, which he has continued to follow through life. In 1859 he emigrated from his native State to Iowa, where he made his home up to 1864, when he removed to Missouri and located in the county whose interests are intrusted to his charge in the present House. A Union man during the late war, he went into the army and served for eight months as a lieutenant in the 34th Iowa regiment. Since a resident of Missouri he has applied himself assiduously to the practice of his profession, only abandoning it to accept a seat in the popular branch of the Twenty-sixth Assembly. Politically, a zealous Democrat, he has, however, in no instance permitted mere party considerations to intefere with his duties as a legislator. Both during session hours and as a member of the Committees on Elections and County Boundaries, he has applied himself earnestly and faithfully to the discharge of the duties devolving upon him.

HENRY SMITH,

The gentleman from Clay, who is among the younger members of the House, was born in the county it has devolved upon him to represent in the present Assembly, October 28th, 1845, his grandfather having removed from New York to that locality at an early day. After attending the common schools of his native county for a number of years, he finally entered William Jewell College at Liberty, in which institution he remained up to 1861, standing at the head of all his classes. In 1862 he removed to the neighboring State of Kansas and engaged in mercantile pursuits, residing there up to the spring of 1863, when he made a trip with a government train across the plains to New Mexico. Returning home in the fall of the same year, he entered the University of Michigan, from which institution he graduated with the bacheloric degree in 1866. From the same institution he also received the degree of master of arts in 1870. Resuming his residence in Kansas on completing his studies, he at once entered the political arena, and was a member of several county and State conventions, and a candidate for the Legislature from the county in which he resided. In the meantime having commenced the study of the law, he was in 1867 admitted to the Kansas bar. In the same year he returned to his native county, locating in the town of Liberty, where he is at present engaged in the practice of his profession, and where he held the office of city attorney for the years 1869 and 1870. Elected a member of the present

House as a Liberal Republican, he has been a consistent member of that party, though never permitting political considerations to interfere with his duties as a Representative. Besides taking a prominent part in the deliberations of the body, being frequently on the floor and always voting with good judgment, he has also served efficiently as a member of the important Committees on the Judiciary and Education, and various special committees. Mr. Smith has just been appointed by Gov. Brown and confirmed by the Senate a member of the Board of Curators of the State University, a position for which he is eminently qualified.

E. J. SORRELL.

The Democratic Representative of the county of Maries, is a native of the Old Dominion, though a resident of Missouri and the county he represents sufficiently long to have become thoroughly acquainted with their interests and institutions. Born in the year 1833, he is still in the prime of life. A merchant by calling, he has nevertheless at all times taken a lively interest in public affairs, and been an active politician. Elected to a seat in the present House in the fall of 1870, his course since at the Capital has been marked by close attention to his duties and their faithful performance according to the convictions of his own conscience. Though making no pretensions as an orator, he never fails to give expression to his views when impelled by considerations of duty to do so. Besides his services during session hours, he has acted as chairman of the Committee on Permanent Seat of Government and a member of a number of important special committees.

JOHN P. STANCIL,

The member from Pemiscot, was born in what is now that county in 1841, his father, Judge Marlin L. Stancil, having immigrated from Tennessee to that locality during the preceding year. At that time the extreme southeastern portion of the State was a comparative wilderness, sparsely populated and without either society, schools or churches. The employment of the inhabitants was divided between the cultivation of their newly-opened farms and the hunt, the one supplying them with bread and the other being their only reliance for meat. Born in this newly settled and scarcely civilized country, the present Representative had the further misfortune of losing his father when only fourteen years of age, after which bereavement he was thrown entirely on his own resources. It being his good fortune, however, to have an intelligent mother, he received at her hands the rudiments of an education, and was enabled to make such progress in his studies that in 1857 he was admitted to the junior class of Clarksville College, in Tennessee, in which he took the first rank in scholarship, and from which he graduated with distinguished honors. After completing his collegiate course he commenced the study of medicine, to which he applied himself for eleven months, when the late war breaking out he enlisted in the 14th Tennessee (Confederate) regiment. Going with that command into Western Virginia he was there attacked with a prevailing malady of the camp, which necessitated his abandoning the service. Being honorably discharged by Mr. Benjamin, then Confederate Secretary of War, he at once returned to his native county, where he continued to reside up to the restoration of peace. In 1866, having in the meantime married and taken possession of his father's farm, he resumed the study of medicine, and in 1867 and 1868 attended the Missouri Medical College at St. Louis, from which, after only one course of lectures, he graduated with honor. On graduating, he at once commenced the practice of his profession in his native county, which he has since continued to follow. Having secured in the highest degree the confidence and respect of his fellow citizens, he was, in 1870, elected by a highly complimentary majority to a seat in the present House, his opponent in the contest being his Democratic predecessor in the Twenty-fifth Assembly. His course since at the Capital has been marked by close application and a faithful performance of the duties devolving upon him, and at all times a conscientious regard for the best interests of his immediate constituency. Though quiet and reserved, there are few members on the Democratic side of the chamber more intelligent or better deserving the trust imposed upon them.

D. K. STEELE,

Occupying a seat in the popular branch of the Twenty-fourth, Twenty-fifth, and now of the Twenty-sixth Assembly, the worthy member from Cooper, though a young man, is a veteran legislator, and fully comprehends all the duties and obligations which the Representative owes to the represented. Mr. Steele is a native Missourian, and was born in the county in which he at present resides, August 31st, 1831. During the late war he served gallantly as a Federal soldier for three years, and was promoted from a private in the ranks to Major. Politically, an Old-Line Whig, so long as that party was in existence, he has under the new order of things been a consistent and conscientious Republican. He has in the present Assembly served as a member of the responsible Committee on Accounts.

GEO. W. SQUIRES,

Representing the county of Henry, is notable as being the oldest member of the House. He was born in Athens county, Ohio, February 15th, 1802, and has therefore reached the allotted age of man. In 1818, being then a lad of sixteen, he commenced steamboating on the Ohio river between the cities of Pittsburgh and Louisville, on the first steamer ever launched on that stream. After following this calling for eighteen years, he immigrated to Missouri and located in what is now Henry but was then Reeves county. At that date this locality was comparatively a wilderness, sparsely inhabited and infested with Indians and wild beasts. In 1837, the year following his locating in his new home, Mr. Squires took command of a company against the Osage Indians, and a year later, commanded a second company against the Mormons, then at Fair West, where he assisted in taking the prophet Jo Smith a prisoner. In 1850 he made an overland trip to California in charge of one of the largest trains which, up to that date, had crossed the plains. After a sojourn of two years in the gold regions, he returned again to Missouri, engaged in steamboating on the Osage river, and did much to open navigation on that stream. In 1858, leaving the river, he went upon a farm in Henry county, and was for a time extensively engaged in raising and selling stock in the Southern market. On the outbreak of the late war he retired to his farm and remained thereon up to the restoration of peace. Though advanced in years, his present seat in the House is the only civil office to which he has aspired or has ever held. While the oldest member of the body, however, he is a scarcely less attentive or active participant in its deliberations than the youngest of his associates. His excellent judgment on all matters have, aside from his years, secured for him almost universal respect at the Capital. Politically, he is a life-long Democrat, having cast his first Presidential vote for Jackson. He has been a valuable member of the Committee on Banks and Corporations.

JOHN L. THOMAS.

The responsible duties devolving upon the chairman of the Committee on Judiciary renders it important in the highest degree that the gentleman for the position should be acquainted thoroughly with the statutory laws, competent to detect their defects and ready to provide the remedy where their operations have shown a change to be required. The peculiar condition in which the present Assembly has found the laws enacted by past Legislatures and affected by the recent amendments to and modification of the Constitution, has rendered the labors of the Judiciary committee of the sitting House of an especially laborious and delicate character, and its chairmanship even a more important post than it has been for many years. The Speaker has, however, found a gentleman in every respect equal to the emergency in the person of Judge Thomas, the accomplished, clear-headed and indefatigable Representative of the county of Jefferson. Few gentlemen have had a more onorous task imposed upon them, and none, I am sure, have applied themselves more faithfully to its discharge. Judge Thomas is a native of that portion of the State now known as Iron county, where he was born in September, 1833. His parents, who were poor, subsequently removed to Washington county, where they resided until 1845, when they removed to Jefferson county, his present home. In the fall of the same year his father died, leaving him at the age of twelve years to manage a small farm for the support of his widowed mother. After remaining in his new home about five years, he removed with his mother to Arcadia, where he entered the Arcadia High School and applied himself diligently to laying the foundation of the excellent education which he has since acquired. Here he remained at school up to 1853, when he graduated from the institution and went out into the world to battle for life without a dollar in his pocket. For two years he taught a village school, and, meantime, applied himself to the study of the law at such intervals of leisure as his duties as a teacher permitted. In the following year he was admitted to the bar, and commenced the practice of his profession in Crawford county. The next year he returned to Jefferson county where he has since resided, and which he now represents in the present House. Starting in life without education or money, he has by his own unaided efforts mastered his profession and established himself in a large and constantly increasing practice. Uniting with his fine abilities as a lawyer a genial disposition and suavity of manner, few members are more esteemed or more popular among his associates. A ready and fluent speaker, he commands the attention of the House, and by his logic and force of argument seldom fails to carry conviction to the minds of his audience.

E. W. TURNER,

The clear-headed and wide-awake member from Clinton, was born in Plattsburg, in that county, November 26th, 1845. After receiving a good common school education, he entered the composing room of the county newspaper published in his native village, from which he graduated a master of "the art preservative." After acquiring his trade he removed to Kansas, and for a short time worked at the "case" in the office of the *Enquirer*, published at Leavenworth City, in that State. Leaving Kansas, he next visited St. Louis, where he remained for several months in the office of the *Free Press*, performing the duties of a clerk. From St. Louis he proceeded to Louisville, Ky., where, after setting type for several months, he obtained more congenial employment as a clerk in one of the larger hotels of that city. Remaining in Louisville up to 1866, he returned in that year to Missouri and settled again in his native county, where he at once commenced the study of the law, and where he is at present engaged in the practice of that profession. In the fall of 1870 receiving the nomination for the Legislature, he was elected to the seat he has filled with credit and efficiency in the present House. Politically, Mr. Turner is a Democrat of the Jefferson school, and is noted as standing almost alone among his party associates at the Capital in opposition to the so-called Missouri or Passive policy. As a speaker, he is ready, fluent and logical, and as a legislator honest, laborious and practical. No member enjoys greater personal popularity either at home or at the Capital.

CHARLES VAN RODEN,

Representing the great mineral county of Iron, was born in Hanover, March 8, 1826. After serving for a number of years in the army of his native country, he immigrated in 1858 to the United States and settled in Iron county, in this State, where he built and occupied the first house where at the present time stands the town of Pilot Knob. Since in his new home he has at different periods followed various avocations, being at present engaged in merchandising. His first and only office is his seat in the popular branch of the present Assembly, to which he was elected as a Liberal Republican. Comprehending thoroughly the important interests of his county, he has faithfully represented them at the Capital, and has therein discharged to the satisfaction of his constituency the special obligations resting upon him. Besides his labors during session hours, he has also served efficiently as a member of the Committees on Mines and Mining, Banks and Corporations and Immigration.

OSCAR VON KOCHTITZKY.

A native of Hungary, a student of the military academy of Dresden, the member of a German army corps in the memorable campaign into Schleswig-Holstein in the spring of 1848, a revolutionist in Hungary under Kossuth in the fall of the same year, an exile in Turkey up to 1850, an emigrant to America, and an officer in the Federal service in the late war between the States in this country, and lastly, Cincinnatus-like, a plain and frugal farmer in Missouri, the life of no member in either chamber of the Capital has probably been so eventful, or would better serve as the foundation of a romance than that of the Democratic Representative of the county of Laclede. But with all this varied experience, his contact with all classes of people, there is probably no more modest or unaffected member of the body in which he sits, than Mr. Von Kochtitzky. Always present in his seat when questions of interest are before the House, and closely attentive to what is going on around him, his vote is invariably cast with intelligence and a rigid regard to his own convictions. A member of the Committee on Agriculture, and several important special committees, and chairman of the Committees on Militia and on Immigration, he has devoted himself to the more responsible duties of the committee room with assiduity, but on the floor of the House he seldom, if ever, seeks to make himself heard when it does not devolve directly upon him to do so, and never engages in petty squabbles over insignificant matters. He both writes and speaks the English perfectly, and there are probably few better educated members in the body. In personal appearance Mr. Von Kochtitzky is about the average hight, of symmetrical and erect figure, and with something of the military in his carriage and address. He has an honest and attractive face, rather of the Teutonic mold, sandy hair and a beard slightly tinged with gray.

JOHN R. WALKER.

Mr. Walker is notable as being the youngest member of the House, having been born in Cooper county, in this State, March 18th, 1846. He is also probably one of the best educated members of the body. After a thorough academic course he completed his studies at the famous school of Yale, and on leaving that institution and returning to Missouri, removed to Bates county, where he has since been engaged in farming and stock-raising, and by whose people he was chosen the guardian of their interests in the present Assembly. On the organization of the House he was assigned by Speaker Wilson to the chairmanship of the important Committee on Elections, the duties of which he has discharged with marked fidelity, impartiality and promptness. He has also done service as a member of the Committees on Printing and the Blind Asylum. Though he is seldom a participant in the debates, it is certainly from no lack of opinions or the ability to express them. Mr. Walker is a Democrat of the strictest school.

J. F. WIELANDY,

The member from Cole, was born in Geneva, Switzerland, in the year 1830, and received his education in the best schools of his native country and Germany. Immigrating to the United States in 1849 he located in Madison county, Illinois, where he purchased and settled upon a farm, though a short time thereafter compelled to abandon that occupation on account of feeble health. On quitting his farm he studied law in Elmira, New York, and on being admitted to the bar commenced the practice of that profession in Illinois, which he continued up to 1859, when he removed to St. Louis. At the outbreak of the late war he entered the army as adjutant of the 2d Missouri regiment, and with his command served under Gen. Lyon throughout the memorable campaign in the Southwest, which culminated in the battle of Wilson's Creek. Leaving the service in 1863, he removed to Jefferson City, where he has since continued to make his home. Under the administration of President Johnson he was appointed Register of the Government Land Office at Boonville, but the Senate failing to confirm the appointment, he held this position for only a few months. He has for a number of years been a member of the State Board of Agriculture, and is at present Secretary of that body. He was also appointed a Curator of the State University by Governor Brown in 1871, and still holds that office. He holds his seat in the present House by a majority of 300 over the united votes of three opposing candidates. Politically, Mr. Wielandy is a Democrat, having cast his first presidential vote for Mr. Buchanan in 1856, though during the war a consistent Unionist. Abandoning the practice of the law in 1864, he has since that date given his time to farming, and more particularly to the cultivation of fruit. He speaks and writes several of the languages with ease, and is an almost constant contributor to Colman's *Rural World* and other agricultural journals, and is also an occasional writer for the political press. As a member of the House, he has distinguished himself by close attention to and the prompt discharge of his duties, and by his services as chairman of the Committee on Agriculture.

J. C. WHITE,

The estimable gentleman representing the county of Texas in the present House, is fifty-four years of age, and a native of Tennessee, though a residence of many years in the Southwestern portion of this State has thoroughly identified him with the people and interests of that section. A farmer by calling, he has never sought official position, and his preferment in the present instance is attributable rather to solicitation of his friends and his personal popularity in his county, than to any wish or effort on his own part. Mr. White is politically a Democrat, and has acted consistently with his party associates in the House in all political questions, though in no instance permitting mere partisanship to govern his action as a legislator. He is among the quiet, but also among the most useful members of the body. He was assigned by the Speaker to the Committee on Federal Relations, and has faithfully discharged the duties devolving on him in that connection.

S. A. WIGHT.

The Southwest has sent no clearer-headed, more faithful or indefatigable member to the present House than the worthy Representative of Vernon county. Few members have answered to more roll calls, and none certainly have voted with better judgment or more strictly in accordance with their convictions of duty and the best interests of their constituency. Mr. Wight is a native of New York, having been born in St. Lawrence county, of that State, October 4th, 1840. After receiving a thoroughly academic education he applied himself to the study of the law, reading for a time in the office of Mr. Wynn, a prominent attorney of Watertown, in his native State, and subsequently attending the law school at Albany, from which institution he graduated with the first honors. On completing his studies he was admitted to practice in his native county, and shortly thereafter removed to the West, locating at Nevada City, his present home in Vernon county, where he at once took the first rank at the bar, and has secured a large and lucrative practice. Before leaving the East he entered and served gallantly for two years as a private soldier in the army of the Potomac; at the end of that time receiving an honorable discharge. Politically, a zealous Democrat, he has done much toward strengthening his party in his adopted county, and as a recognition of his services in this particular he was the almost unanimous choice of his party associates for the nomination which resulted in his election to a seat in the present Assembly. Of his course at the Capital I have already spoken. While a ready, fluent and logical debater, he never speaks for mere effect, and has entirely refrained from indulgence in the more frivolous discussions of the session. The author of several important measures, he has been untiring in their support, while he has done excellent service as a member of the important Committees on Ways and Means, Criminal Jurisprudence, Township Organization, Constitutional Amendments and the Judicial Redistricting of the State.

R. S. WILKS,

Representing the county of Lawrence, is a native of Tennessee, in which State he was born in 1833. During his youth his parents removed to Missouri locating in Lawrence county, where he has since continued to make his home, and where he is at present engaged in the occupation of farming. Entering the army at the outbreak of the late war, he served to the close with the rank of Major. Politically, Mr. Wilks is a Republican, though his course at the Capital has been such as to make for him friends in all parties. Few gentlemen are personally more popular among their immediate friends. Always observant of the proceedings of the body, he has taken an intelligent part therein, and invariably voted with good judgment on all questions. He has also done efficient service as a member of the Committee on Immigration, and on a number of the more important special committees.

H. WILLIAMS,

The member from Audrain, is a native of the Old North State, having been born in Gates county, of that commonwealth, February 12th, 1821. In 1831 his parents immigrated to Missouri, and were among the first settlers in Callaway county, in this State. After a residence of twenty-four years in Callaway, Mr. Williams removed to Mexico, his present home in Audrain county, where he has since continued to reside. He has from boyhood up been engaged in mercantile pursuits, having commenced as a clerk and subsequently embarking in business for himself. His sterling business habits, strict probity and pleasant manners, have made for him friends wherever he has resided, and have frequently resulted in his preferment to local office. The present, however, is, I believe, the first official position he has ever held that has called him away from his private pursuits. Politically, Mr. Williams is a zealous and uncompromising

7*

Democrat. Since a member of the Assembly he has, besides his services during session hours, been a laborious member of the important Committees on Ways and Means and the Deaf and Dumb Asylum.

J. W. WILLIAMS,

In whom the county of Morgan has found a laborious and conscientious Representative, is a native of Kentucky, having been born in Adair county, in that State, January 25th, 1824. When an infant his parents removed to the neighboring State of Tennessee, where they remained up to 1838, when they removed to Greene county, in this State, where the early manhood of the present Representative was spent on a farm. Residing here up to 1862, he removed in that year to Dallas county, in the following year to Polk county, and thence to Illinois in 1864. Remaining in Illinois only one year, he returned to Missouri, and after a brief sojourn in Cooper county finally settled in the county where he at present resides, and by whose people he has been honored with a seat in the present Assembly. A farmer by calling, he has also united with that avocation the duties of a minister of the gospel of the Missionary Baptist faith. Politically, an Old-Line Whig, he has since the dissolution of that party been a zealous Republican. As a member of the House he has been assiduous in the discharge of his duties, seldom absent from his seat and always prepared to vote with good judgment. The only committee on which he has done service has been that on Elections, the duties of which were chiefly performed during the regular session.

ROBERT F. WINGATE.

Mr. Stone, who, a lucrative appointment under the administration of Mayor Brown, induced to resign his seat as Representative of the Eleventh district of St. Louis, is succeeded in the adjourned session of the House by a gentleman of scarcely less distinguished abilities, though of widely different political tenets. General Wingate was born in Boone county, Kentucky, January 24th, 1822, and removed with his parents to Gallatin county, Illinois, in 1834, where he worked on a farm for four years. At the expiration of this time he left the parental roof, and with only three dollars in his pocket, made his way to Mt. Vernon, in Jefferson county, of that State, where he attended school, supporting himself in the meantime by working mornings and nights at such employment as he could manage to find. Having by this means acquired a fair scholastic education, he removed to Columbus, Indiana, where he commenced the study of the law in the office of a relative residing at that place. Prosecuting his studies here until admitted to the bar, he returned to Mt. Vernon and commenced the practice of his profession, which he continued to follow until 1853, when he removed to St. Louis, where he is still engaged in the practice, and where, by application, industry and frugality, he has acquired a handsome fortune. In 1862 he was elected from the district he at present represents to a seat in the popular branch of the Assembly. While a member of that body, he introduced a resolution instructing our Congressmen to propose an amendment to the Federal Constitution abolishing the institution of slavery throughout the States, this being the first time that such a measure had been proposed, and it is worthy of note that the very amendment subsequently adopted is in language identically that first suggested by the present Representative. Having filled his seat in the House up to 1864, he was in that year elected Attorney General of the State, in which capacity he continued to serve up to 1869. At the same time he also served as a judge advocate under appointment of the Governor. On the expiration of his official term he returned to the practice of his profession in St. Louis, to which he continued to devote himself up to his election to a seat in the present House. Preceded by a reputation achieved in the earlier days of his legislative experience, Mr. Wingate assumed at once a position second to none of his associates on the Republican side of the chamber, in which his course throughout the present session has fully sustained him. With a fine command of language, acute reasoning powers, and a naturally logical mind, he has taken an active part in the debates of the body, and never fails to command the respectful attention of his audience.

CUSTIS WORDEN,

Whose name occurs last on the roll of the House, and who represents in the present Assembly the county of Cass, is a New Yorker, having been born in Chenango county, in that State, July 20th, 1820, where he was raised on a farm. Immigrating to the West in 1840, he located first in Ohio, subsequently in Illinois, and finally settled in the county whose interests have been intrusted to his charge in the present House. Adopting the calling of a farmer when a boy, he has followed that independent avocation through life in connection with stock raising, in which he is at present extensively engaged. The only official trust he has ever sought or had imposed upon him, is that which he holds at this time in the House. In politics, he was an Old-Line Whig so long as that party was in existence, and since its dissolution he has been a zealous and consistent Republican. Among the more reticent members of the body in which he sits, he has, nevertheless, been a hard-worker throughout the session, seldom absent from his seat, and closely observant of all that transpires in the hall. He has also done valuable service as a member of the Committee on Township Organization and the Committee on Accounts.

THE CORRESPONDENTS' TABLE.

MAJ. JOHN N. EDWARDS.

This gentleman, who, in conjunction with Mr. Regan, is Public Printer of the House, as well as Capital correspondent of the Kansas City *Times*, was born in Farquhar county, Virginia, and was educated in Washington City. He learned the printer's art in Lexington, Missouri. At the beginning of the war he entered the Confederate service as a private. Though unpretentious and retiring, he was rapidly promoted, and soon became Major General Joe Shelby's Adjutant General. Of his military life, it is sufficient to say that it was brilliant and unstained by a single act unworthy a soldier. At the conclusion of the war, with some comrades-in-arms, he went to the city of Mexico, where for two years he edited a newspaper in the imperial interest. The fall of Maximilian caused Maj. Edwards' return to Missouri, where he procured a position on the staff of the Missouri *Republican*. He there wrote the book entitled "Shelby and his Men." He next became an assistant editor of the Kansas City *Times*, but after a brief service became chief editor of that influential journal. He spends his winters at Jefferson City as correspondent of his paper. As a newspaper correspondent, it is safe to say that he is unsurpassed in this State and probably in this country. His style is pure, graceful and terse. His letters are full of humor, his sketches are vivid and racy, and there is a quaintness of imagery and warmth of sentiment that remind you of the aromatic sweetness of the nosegay.

WILLIAM FAYEL,

The correspondent of the Missouri *Republican*, and the best known of all the newspaper gentlemen at the Capital, was born in Otsego county, New York. During his youth he enjoyed the advantages of the best schools of his section, and early developed a passion for books, which have given him, in his maturer years, a rich store of varied and useful information. In 1852, having taken some part in previous political campaigns, he was induced to make a race for the Legislature on the Whig ticket in Jefferson county, of his native State. Fortunately, perhaps, he was defeated, as his well-known independence of character would have been a bar against promotion in political life. A portion of 1853 he passed in Washington City as correspondent of the Black River *Journal*, and this was his first introduction into newspaper life. In 1855 he purchased an interest in the Lockport (Niagara county) *Journal*, and his active journalistic career dates from this period. His paper was Whig, but shortly became Republican in politics—the former party being merged into the latter. He was one of seven who recommended, in an address, a union of the two parties in Niagara county, although it is surmised that, in later years, he was not very proud of the vote he cast, in 1856, for the so-called "Pathfinder," Fremont. Mr. Fayel remained in the Lockport *Journal* until about the commencement of the late war, and great popular demonstrations were being made all over the State against those who sympathized with the South. Several of the Democratic newspaper establishments in his vicinity were mobbed, and their editors compelled to flee to Canada. The Lockport *Daily Advertiser* and *Niagara Democrat* were threatened, and its editor besought Mr. Fayel to save his establishment. The request was complied with by Mr. F., who immediately hoisted the stars and stripes over the office and thus placed the paper on an intensely loyal basis. In July, 1861, Mr. Fayel arrived in St. Louis, and immediately attached himself to the Missouri *Democrat* as its war correspondent. He was with Curtis on his Southwest and Arkansas campaigns. His letters, over his own signature of "Fayel," were read with great interest, and republished in most of the principal papers of the country. After Gen. Curtis' campaigns, Mr. Fayel settled in St. Louis, where, for four or five years, he filled the position of local editor, respectively, of the *Daily Union* and the *Daily Evening News*. In 1867 he became permanently employed on the Missouri *Republican* as a local writer and correspondent, and his letters from the Indian country to that journal greatly enhanced his former brilliant reputation as a letter writer. In 1867-8 he accompanied the Indian Peace Commission, visiting nearly all of the Indian tribes on the Upper Missouri and the Southern tribes at Medicine Lodge Creek, writing most interesting letters, descriptive of scenery, savage life and passing events, to his paper. In 1870 he went with a committee of the Board of Indian Commissioners, acting as secretary of the committee—Mr. Felix Bruno and Col. Robert Campbell—and the *Republican's* correspondent. During the following autumn, he accompanied Commissioners Campbell, Long and Farwell to the great Indian Council at Okmulgee, in the same dual position. It is sufficient to say that the Commissioners, in making up their reports, drew largely on Mr. Fayel's correspondence, while his letters were extensively republished all over the country, and regarded as good authority by high officials and those interested in the character and status of the "gentlemen without hats," as Mr. Fayel facetiously styled them. For ten winters Mr. Fayel has attended the sessions of the Missouri Legislature in the capacity of correspondent, and all connected with the General Assembly and Executive departments respect him for his splendid capacity, his great moral worth and kind and genial nature.

GEORGE W. GILSON.

Major Gilson, the well-known correspondent at the Capital of the Missouri *Democrat,* was born in 1832, near Cleveland, Ohio. In 1840, during the "hard cider campaign," he, with his father, accompanied Tom. Corwin, Thomas L. Ewing, and other Whig orators of that day, in a stumping tour over the State. Perched on cider barrels, vast political assemblages were treated to oratorical harangues and campaign songs, in which young Gilson, though a mere stripling, was a welcome amateur. At eleven years of age he was an apprentice in a printing establishment, where, during a term of four years, he became a proficient in the business, and at the age of fifteen served as journeyman, thus becoming fully versed in the practical workings of journalism. The Mexican war was raging at this time, and though still a mere youth, his patriotic ambition was fired, and he went as a private soldier in the army of invasion of our neighboring Republic. His father sought to oppose his going, and being an Old-Line Whig, appealed to the Secretary of War, and even demanded of Gen. Scott, with whom he had served as captain of cavalry in 1812, the immediate discharge from the army of his youthful son. Young Gilson was attached to a battalion of regulars, which comprised a portion of the garrison at Puebla for several months. He spent nearly a year with the army, having in the meantime marched with the invaders into the City of Mexico. Having participated thus gallantly with the defenders of his country as sergeant of his company, he returned home. He came to Missouri in 1850, since which time, with the exception of three years service in the late war, he has passed his time in this State, engaged in various newspaper offices as printer, foreman, publisher and editor. In 1857 he filled the position of superintendent of the Missouri *Statesman,* at Columbia, under the veteran, Col. Switzler. The next year, 1858, was passed in Kansas City as editor and publisher of the Western *Metropolitan,* a paper of Free State proclivities. For several years past Maj. Gilson has been connected with the Missouri *Democrat,* holding positions on the reportorial and editorial staff of that widely known and popular journal. In these varied capacities he has won a marked influence as an enterprising correspondent and able writer. As a journalist, Maj. Gilson wields a fluent pen, and his great experience, fine taste and excellent judgment renders him an invaluable attache to a "live newspaper." During the war, Maj. Gilson held several commissions in the service. In 1864, and part of 1865, he filled the position of Inspector General of the St. Louis military district, then embracing a territory which took in all of St. Louis and Southeast Missouri. In this position he won high commendation from his superiors and the War Department. Honorable mention and the appointment by brevet to Brigadier General was tendered.

JOHN W. PATTISON,

House reporter of the Missouri *Republican*, was born in Fairfield county, Connecticut, in 1834, is now thirty-eight years of age, and a graduate of the Wesleyan University. At twenty years of age, he assumed the editorial management of the S. W. *Advocate*, Gov. Floyd's home organ, at Tazewell Court House, Virginia. Early in the summer of 1854 he migrated to Omaha, Nebraska, and started the first paper in that territory, the "Omaha *Arrow*," and assisted materially in adding to the prosperity of that section. During the years of 1855-6 he was the spicy frontier correspondent of the New York *Herald* and *Times*, and then again editor of the Omaha *Times*. He was a captain of a volunteer infantry in the early Indian troubles in Nebraska, and was deputy and acting U. S. Marshal of the territory. In 1859 he started the Southwestern *Iowan*, a successful Democratic paper at Sidney, Fremont county, Iowa, where he remained until the second year of the war, when he joined the Federal forces, and served with credit until the close of the war. Then he became city editor of the Quincy (Ill.) Daily *Herald*, and afterward editor of the Quincy Evening *Journal*. Later, he was editor of a live Democratic paper at Savannah, "The *Union*," in Andrew county, and about three years ago joined the reportorial force of the Missouri *Republican*. Latterly, he has become part proprietor of the Boonville *Advertiser*, a leading Democratic paper of Central Missouri. Mr. Pattison has had some sixteen years' experience of successful editorial life, is a spicy, agreeable writer, brim-full of progress, and thoroughly devoted to the growth and interest of the Great West, over which he has extensively traveled. He is a staunch Democrat, a man of family, and has a host of friends throughout the West.

JAMES HOLLAND,

Correspondent of the Missouri *Democrat*, was born in Dublin, Ireland, in the year 1846, and is consequently now twenty-six years of age. He attended the school of Dublin until the year 1861, when he became secretary to Lord Digby, in London. After remaining with this nobleman about three years, Mr. Holland left England for the Cape of Good Hope, and passed some time in Southern Africa, engaging in elephant and ostrich hunting and traveling through the countries of the Hotentots, Kaffirs, Damaras and Bushman. Finally leaving Africa and afterward visiting the Island of St. Helena, he came to the United States in 1868, and, after traveling in different parts of the country, eventually settled in St. Louis in the latter part of 1869, where, after some time, he entered into a business partnership with Mr. L. L. Walbridge, of St. Louis, forming the firm of short-hand writers, known under the title of Walbridge & Holland. Mr. Holland is one of the most accomplished short-hand writers in the country, and in reporting the proceedings of the House for the paper he represents, has exhibited remarkable ability in his profession.

STANLEY WATERLOO.

Mr. Waterloo has been a correspondent at the Capital for various newspapers, but he represents more particularly the St. Louis *Journal of Commerce*, as its political writer. His comments of legislative doings are characterized by a raciness, mixed with a sprinkling of dry humor. He was born in St. Clair, Michigan, in 1846. The first fifteen years of his life were passed on a farm. In 1861 he engaged in mercantile pursuits, and kept a store on the line of the Grand Trunk railroad, in the State of Michigan. This pursuit he followed about a year, and then prepared for college. He entered the University of Michigan in 1865, and engaged in teaching a short time thereafter, and in the latter part of 1869 came to Chicago. In that city he spent six months in studying law, and during spare intervals, did Bohemian work on the city newspapers. He engaged as reporter on the Evening *Post*, but after a short time left that paper to become associate editor on the Insurance *Spectator*, owned by the Goodsells. In 1870 he left the *Spectator* and assumed the editorship of the American *Builder*, a technical magazine devoted to the advancement of the profession indicated by the title. The position was congenial with his tastes. The articles emanating from his pen, are his specialty, were republished in this country and England. He remained thus engaged until the Great Fire obliged him, like hundreds of others, to seek another home. He came to publish the *Builder* in St. Louis after the fire, but was offered a position as a political writer on the *Journal of Commerce*, which offer was accepted. Mr. Waterloo is still in the summer of life—being twenty-six years of age—and with his ability and capacity for work has a brilliant future before him.

G. W. FRAME,

One of the representatives at the Capital of the St. Louis *Times* during the adjourned session, is a native of Missouri, having been born in Daviess county, February 18th, 1850. He is, therefore, the youngest member of the correspondents' and reportorial corps of the House. After receiving a good education, he turned his attention to journalism, and in 1867 purchased the Gallatin *Democrat,* which he conducted successfully for two years. After this, he became attached to the staff of the Kansas City *Evening News*, and subsequently of the *Times* of the same city. An easy and racy writer, and still quite young, he gives promise of making his mark in his profession.

Printed in Dunstable, United Kingdom